What would the SPICE GIRLS do?

HOW THE GIRL POWER GENERATION GREW UP

LAUREN BRAVO

BANTAM PRESS

LONDON · TORONTO · SYDNEY · AUCKLAND · JOHANNESBURG

TRANSWORLD PUBLISHERS
61–63 Uxbridge Road, London W5 5SA
www.penguin.co.uk

Transworld is part of the Penguin Random House group
of companies whose addresses can be found at
global.penguinrandomhouse.com

Penguin
Random House
UK

First published in Great Britain in 2018 by Bantam Press
an imprint of Transworld Publishers

A CIP catalogue record for this book
is available from the British Library.

ISBN 9781787631304

Typeset in Helvetica Neue Light. Designed by Julia Lloyd.
Printed and bound in Great Britain by Clays Ltd, Elcograf S.p.A.

Penguin Random House is committed to a sustainable
future for our business, our readers and our planet. This book is
made from Forest Stewardship Council® certified paper.

MIX
Paper from
responsible sources
FSC® C019777

1 3 5 7 9 10 8 6 4 2

For Jo, Hannah, Rose,
Lizzie and Sarah.

And all the
Ace Gangs everywhere.

CONTENTS

'If you'd asked at the time, I'd have said the Spice Girls were a trivial distraction. Now, I'm not so sure. I think they were quite pivotal for our generation, actually.'

CLARE, 30

INTRODUCTION

Usually, when you say you 'came of age' during something, it means adolescence. You think of high school movies, teen angst, disappointing proms, lots of drinking in parks and non-specific yearning out of bus windows.

But when I say I came of age during the reign of the Spice Girls, I mean that I was eight when 'Wannabe' was released. The perfect age for the fandom, albeit a weird one to be singing about lovers. I turned nine in 1997, a year notable for so many things but not least for being the Spice Girls' Year of Glory, in which they went eight times platinum, became film stars, wooed Nelson Mandela, won two Brit Awards and made a Union Jack tea towel one of the most iconic outfits in music history. I was ten (it really was only two years later) when Geri left the group and burst pop's biggest bubble since Beatlemania.

Those years spanned, as my friend Alice puts it poetically, 'that golden period of girlhood'. The halcyon days – and the best ones, it turns out, for an all-consuming pop star obsession. When you're looking for an easy foothold in adulthood. You're too young to know how complicated the world is, but just old enough to feel like you can conquer it.

Of course, that feeling fades. I started secondary school as we stared down a new century, and finished university in the chaos of a global recession – at that point we still called it, adorably, the 'credit crunch'. And this means I'm every inch a millennial now; a card-carrying, app-reliant, slogan-toting, overambitious snowflake who can't do mental maths any more. But I'm something else too. A graduate of the girl power generation.

Once, nostalgia seemed the preserve of crusty oldsters; now, like all Spice Age alumni, I get high on the memory of Sunny D and inflatable furniture. Misty-eyed for a time when 'influence' meant a *Smash Hits* interview, and we coveted a Dream Phone rather than being ruled by a smart one. A time when being British was regarded as cool and exciting, not something murky and fractious to be apologized for on a European city break.

And at the centre of that nineties tableau, five bolshy upstarts in massive shoes, who changed everything. While Clarissa explained it all and only Smarties had the answer, the most pressing question in virtually every situation became, 'What would the Spice Girls do?' Little did we know so many of the lessons we were learning then would be the same ones we're still grappling with today.

There's plenty I don't remember about those years. Fractions. The periodic table. What exactly happened at the Battle of Bosworth. Great chunks of my Key Stage 2 education have crumbled away into the ether. But I remember every single detail of Christmas morning 1997 – the heady scent of the Impulse body spray in my stocking, the Dairy Milk selection box I ate for breakfast, and the soundtrack: *Spiceworld*, on cassette, boomed through the house from my bedroom tape player as loud as seasonal goodwill would allow.

I had never owned *Spice*, their first album – only borrowed it from the library for a week at a time. Cost: £1 and the heartbreak of returning it afterwards for some other kid to adore. But now, here, finally, in my hands, was my very own piece of girl power.

Years later, I would learn that *Spice* was the first album my now-boyfriend ever bought, and see this as evidence of our ultimate compatibility. The yin to my yang! PJ to my Duncan! The other half of my mutant CatDog! But that Christmas morning, boys were nowhere on the agenda.

'Chicas to the front!' I sang, attempting a clumsy salsa as I crimped my fringe with my Babyliss 4x4 styler, the smell of turkey wafting up the stairs and mingling with my cloud of synthetic vanilla. I shook it to the right, like they did in the video. I slammed it to the left, and partially into a chest of drawers. I was having a good time.

The previous evening I'd assumed my usual position:

lying flat on my belly on the living-room carpet, nose towards the telly. It was from this vantage point, in May of the same year, that I witnessed the most historic landslide result of my generation – Katrina and the Waves winning Eurovision. I taped it off the telly on VHS and re-watched it every day for a fortnight. It was lying on the carpet, one morning in August, that I flipped, aghast, through five channels announcing the same identical, horrible news, over and over. Princess Diana was dead, dead, dead, still dead, dead again, and all the cartoons had been cancelled.

And it was there again, on Christmas Eve, that I watched Ginger, Scary, Sporty, Baby and Posh perform the second of their three consecutive Christmas number ones. From 'Too Much' I learned lessons that I would apply first to blue raspberry Slush Puppies, then to metallic cream eyeshadow, and finally to relationships. I learned that too much of something is bad enough, but too much of nothing is just as tough. And, more obliquely, that I needed to know the way to feel to keep me satisfied. I still do, let's be honest. It immediately became my second favourite Spice Girls song.

What's my *favourite* Spice Girls song? I'm so glad you asked! It's 'The Lady Is A Vamp'.

I know, I know. In Spice Girls terms this is like telling people your favourite Bowie track is 'The Laughing Gnome'. But I won't apologize, because 'The Lady Is A Vamp' is fabulous. Its camp, ritzy, soft-jazz schtick couldn't have appealed more directly and urgently to my pre-teen self if it had a free snap bracelet attached. The song features a roll call of pop culture icons: Elvis, Ziggy, Marley, Twiggy. Jackie O. Diana Ross. Even a cryptic nod to John Coltrane. It was a sheet of ready-made crib notes for kids at the arse end of the millennium, gagging for their own pop heroes but also for a handle on everything that had gone before.

I would sing along to 'The Lady Is A Vamp' standing on the living-room ottoman in an imaginary gold lamé sheath dress, a chorus of imaginary dancing boys swirling around me. In my head I was part *An Audience with Shirley Bassey*, part Marilyn doing 'Diamonds Are A Girl's Best Friend'. Except I hadn't seen Marilyn's version, or even Madonna's 'Material Girl' homage – I only knew the routine because someone had parodied it on short-lived CBBC sitcom *No Sweat*. That's how it was, being a kid of the nineties. Everything felt like a hand-me-down.

Until the Spice Girls.

Their stratospheric rise to fame might have earned comparisons to sixties and seventies pop hysteria, but they were no retro reboot. And their attitude wasn't about chewing over the past, either – it was brand spanking new. It didn't dwell on the things we weren't; it was a soundtrack for all the things we could be.

I grew up in an era of contradictions. It was the golden age of lads' mags, ladettes and professional socialites, a time that winkingly called itself 'post-feminist' while it pinched the metaphorical arse of the progress that went before it. Many of us were raised by women who had fought for the rights we took for granted – women who remembered a time when abortion was illegal, but sexual harassment and discrimination were not. Women who needed the signature of a husband or father to buy a home or open a bank account. Women who probably weren't sure how to feel about tweeny-bopper daughters who wanted to wear a PVC miniskirt to Tesco. Indie, grunge and riot grrrl fans saw mainstream pop music as the plague, while the old guard of feminists heaped scorn on what they saw as a watered-down, capitalist appropriation of women's lib.

But of course, you don't know any of this stuff when you're eight. You just know what you love. And anyway, the Spice Girls weren't for our mothers, or for Germaine Greer. They were all ours.

The year 1996, according to the first line of its Wikipedia page, is notable for 'the Dunblane Massacre, the divorces of the Duke and Duchess of York and of the Prince and Princess of Wales, the birth of Dolly the sheep, and the breakthrough of the Spice Girls'. There is a bracketed note after the Spice Girls' name that reads '[importance?]'. I reject that note. If you want to know how important the breakthrough of the Spice Girls was, ask all the girls who broke through with them.

Because while the Fab Five dominated the headlines and tabloid front pages, another story was beginning behind the curtains of pre-teen bedrooms across the country – one that continued long after our Polaroid Spice Cams had broken and the dolls had been sent to the charity shop. Now we're fully grown Spice Women in our own right, grappling with adult dilemmas and batting back every curveball the modern world throws our way, the time feels right to re-evaluate their legacy. It's time to ask a few questions.

Questions such as: Why does nobody make up dance routines any more? Can we blame our bad lumbars on the platform boots? What was a 'zig-a-zig-ah', and did they ever get one? Did any of us, in fact? Are we the zig-a-zig-ahless generation? Should we be prioritizing one over our Help to Buy ISAs? But also, the bigger debates. Was girl power a capitalist sham, or was it a feminist launch pad? When will the world stop telling women they're doing everything wrong?

Back then we asked, 'What would the Spice Girls do?', and now, with society two decades older but in many ways barely wiser, so much of their philosophy still feels relevant today. Ahead of its time, even. So, with that in mind, I want to ask instead: What did the Spice Girls do for us?

For one thing, they freed us from the tyranny of simpering boybands and sent oestrogen soaring up the charts like never before. And while it wasn't punk as our parents knew it, the Spice Girls bred their own kind of anarchy. They were fiercely, cheerfully defiant in the face of an industry that sneered at them. 'Manufactured' they may have been, but even at the height of world domination, those women were nobody's puppets.

They had undeniable swagger from the off. This is the

group that fired the managers who created them, badgered songwriters into working with them for free, danced on desks until they snared a record deal, and staged a gutsy 'midnight flit' with all their master recordings hidden in their pants. The group that sacked their Svengali at the peak of their fame and took the reins of their own career.

'It's like six-year-olds driving a lorry,' quipped Geri of that time, an image that sums up imposter syndrome so perfectly I want to emboss it on a notebook I'll never fill.

Don't we all sometimes feel like a six-year-old driving a lorry? And by 'sometimes' I mean often. Daily. Constantly. As a generation, we feel so ill-equipped for adult life that we've had to invent a cutesy noun – 'adulting' – just to make the whole affair feel more like a game and less like cold, hard reality. We're riddled with doubts, habitual second-guessers, confused about what society tells us we should want, and what we actually want. What we really, really want.

But it's also kind of a comfort, in a modern landscape where to express an opinion on anything as a woman is to immediately have a 'Well Actually' pop up and explain why you're wrong, to remember that the Spice Girls were told they did everything wrong too.

I am convinced, for example, that there are better, more talented and more qualified people than me to be writing this book. In fact, I'm sure there are – heaps of them. Maybe you! But every time that I've ended up slumped over my laptop with crisps in my hair, whimpering, 'I can't do it I can't do it I can't do it,' while 'Wannabe' plays on a canny loop, I've tried to remember that there were also heaps of better, more talented and more qualified people than the Spice Girls to be world-famous pop stars. But that never held them back. So here we are.

Inevitably the Spice explosion only burned bright for a short time (like most true fans I barely acknowledge the third album and we do *not* speak of GEM).

Even when the Spices' star began to fade, it happened in scene-stealing fashion. You could argue that Geri leaving the group (an event we'll naturally call 'Gexit') was as much of a baller move as anything else they did. Because quitting *can* be empowering, can't it? I've always loved a good quit. Nothing feels better than jacking in a miserable job and strutting off into the sunset with your head held high. (My £4.80 an hour student gig in a Camden vintage shop might not be strictly comparable to leaving the most successful girl group in history, but while Geri's job involved being hounded daily by paparazzi and bound to a near-inhumane work schedule, I had to wear a bumbag. It's impossible to say which is the bigger cross to bear.)

Besides, the afterglow lives on. 'They made me who I am,' declared Adele in 2011, sending thousands of us racing to Spotify for a nostalgia binge. In more recent years, stars such as Charlie XCX, Ariana Grande and MØ have covered Spice Girls songs, and talked about their formative influence. As all great musical heroes should, the Spices paved a new path and danced us down it.

Years later, I still get a bit teary just thinking about them on the roofs of those London cabs at the 2012 Olympics (actually I get teary as soon as anyone even says 'the 2012 Olympics', but still). It wasn't Live Aid, it wasn't Woodstock, but it was something. A moment. There they were, the ordinary girls done good, proving that even squeaky nineties pop could mean something to somebody.

Above all, I think we still get emotional about the Spice Girls because they were the first true phenomenon that was all our own. The clothes, the poses, the daft made-up words. The money men might have brought them together but we, the fans, made them famous – with every album and tour ticket and branded body spray, we all bought into the cult of Spice, and in many ways we're still reaping returns on that investment today.

We, the girl power generation, who grew up but stayed angry. Who remember the dance routines and the lyrics like it's still Christmas morning 1997. Who sent off a stamped addressed envelope for equality twenty years ago, and still haven't had it delivered. We came of age too young, some people said, and yet plenty of us still feel like we haven't 'come of age' at all. Some of us, let's be honest, would rather still be lying on our bellies on our parents' living-room carpet.

But instead we're here, the former Wannabes, out there being. We're flicking peace signs in our selfies and forming our own girl gangs for support and rebellion. There are those of us who still haven't quite got the glitter gel out of our hair, and plenty of us still haven't quite got the Spice Girls out of our system.

I know this is true, because I've asked. I've surveyed and interviewed more than seventy Spice Girls fans of my generation (and a few beyond). One thing I *do* remember from maths lessons is that it's good to show your workings, so I've included as many of these stories and opinions as possible in the following pages.

It was surprisingly easy – just mention the group and people's stories and opinions come gushing out like warm Capri-Sun. I've heard about the outfits, the merch, the parental battles and the furtive sex ed lessons from the sleeve lyrics. I've been told over and over about the way the Spice Girls made us feel back then, and everything they still mean to us now, when we think about it.

And I've thought about it, a lot. I've revisited the interviews, the videos and the performances. I've re-watched *Spice World* three times, I've listened to the albums on repeat, and I've even done it wearing brown lip liner, just to really be sure.

What have I concluded, about everything those five women meant to my generation? Just like the lip liner, their legacy has lingered on for longer than anyone might have imagined. Here's how.

SPICE GIRLS FOR THE MODERN WORLD!

Flaky Spice

Mindful Spice

Introvert Spice

Woke Spice

Early Adopter Spice

Side Hustle Spice

Self-care Spice

Whistleblower Spice

Snowflake Spice

Shy Tory Spice

Vegan Spice

Off-grid Spice

Pumpkin Spice

'Yes, they were all labelled with different stereotypes – but those different personalities sent a message that girls come in all different shapes and sizes, with different interests and passions. I don't think any other band has really done this for me. Together they made up this one mothership of sass and love.'

THULASY, 30

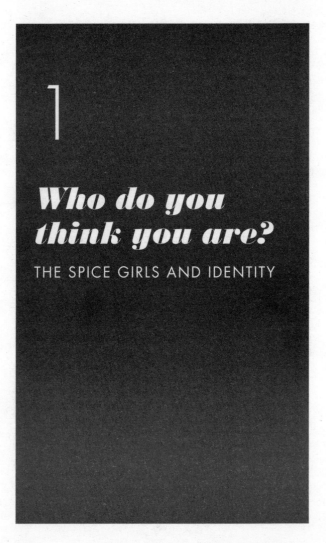

1

Who do you think you are?

THE SPICE GIRLS AND IDENTITY

To be a woman is to be endlessly categorized and taxonomized. Are you an Audrey or a Marilyn? A Charlotte or a Samantha? A Jo March, a Hermione Granger or perhaps a Snorkmaiden from *The Moomins* with Anna Karenina rising? Are you the pink or the yellow Power Ranger? Are you an apple or a pear? Or a handful of pomegranate seeds, shoved into a sock? Which dog are you? Which dog meme are you? Are you a dog meme at all, and if not then WHO EVEN ARE YOU? The quest for identification has plagued our gender for as long as there have been other women or inanimate objects to compare us to.

Back before we had Buzzfeed quizzes to clarify matters, we relied on magazine flowcharts, Bang on the Door pencil cases (whither Groovy Chick?) or just standing in the middle of the school field waiting for somebody to yell an identifier at us. Sometimes being a girl is like sitting on a production line, waiting for society to slap a label on your head and ship you out.

And of course, any Spice Girls fan worth her salt knew exactly which member she 'was' – whether you made the choice yourself or had it forced upon you by group consensus because you had blonde hair/glasses/access to your big sister's Wonderbra. As thousands upon thousands of copycat fivesomes spawned in playgrounds across the world, so commenced the scrabble to claim 'your' Spice, ergo your identity.

For many, they were fraught times. I've heard the stories.

'I really wanted to be Mel C, with her Celtic tattoos, gold tooth and unattainable athleticism, but I couldn't do handstands and that was apparently a requirement to qualify,' says Hannah, one of thousands who carry the mental scars of a miscast Spicedom.

'I wanted to be Emma but I had short dark hair so I *had* to be Posh,' says another, who endured further upset during the S Club 7 years as a result of her passing resemblance to Tina.

One fan tells me she tried to dye the two front sections of her hair with lemon juice, à la Geri. 'It did not work.' (Once upon a time, lemon juice was more than a salad dressing, kids; it was a valuable commodity. Records are inconclusive on how much of the average nineties childhood was spent trying and failing to do things with lemon juice, but mainly because the records are in 'invisible writing' and still drying on a radiator somewhere.)

I, in the precarious position of once-blonde-turned-mousy, was forced to shore up my claim on Ginger with a month's worth of pocket money and an armful of Shaders & Toners colour sachets. Inside, I knew I was Geri. It wasn't even a matter of *wanting* to be her – I'd have fancied a crack at Baby or Posh if my overbearing personality hadn't ruled them out – I simply *was* Geri. To watch some polite, introvert redhead swoop in and snatch her from me would have been too much to bear. I'd have died. So I dyed.

But while hair colour held sway in the playground casting process, it wasn't the only decider – or the most questionable. 'I was usually Scary, because there were no black girls but my stepdad was black, and the other girls figured that was good enough,' one fan tells me.

Author and entrepreneur Otegha Uwagba was a Sporty at heart, but often found herself stepping into Scary's shoes. 'Her representation as a black woman is now, in hindsight, very problematic, but at the time I just thought, "Great! She's black, I'm black,"' Uwagba says. 'Now I look back at the way she was presented as, well, the Scary one – loud and mad, constantly wearing leopard print...There are so many shades of inappropriateness there. But at the time it felt positive.'

'She made me feel OK about having large frizzy hair for the first time,' agrees another juvenile Scary. 'And the last time, actually, until I was an adult.'

For their critics, the Spices' willingness to play up to their set roles – flimsy roles at that – has always been high on the list of reasons to knock them. It's hard to argue. 'Baby' is obviously a problematic nightmare; 'Scary' is rife with inherent prejudice; 'Ginger' isn't a personality trait at all, FFS. Ideally, girls should learn that there are unlimited slots for them to fill in the world, and infinite ways they're allowed to be. In 1996, there were five. Six, if you counted 'refusenik All Saints fan'.

Still, it was more than one – and though it's hard to see it now, the group's delicious pick 'n' mix of personalities made them a breath of fresh air at the time. Most pop groups were styled in homogeneous monotones, their members presented as seamlessly interchangeable and their whole identities boiled down to being 'the blonde' or 'the one on the end'. The Spice Girls did the opposite. To paraphrase RuPaul, who I don't think would mind, they used the whole box of crayons.

It was a smaller box of crayons than we have now, sure. A Woolworths value pack, not the luxury 24-piece Crayola set with the neon watermelon pink. We can hardly call the Spice Girls 'diverse' by today's standards, let's be clear about that – and thank God for progress. But for kids struggling to figure out where they fitted on the flowchart, they offered something a little more hopeful to hold on to at a pivotal age.

'Looking back, they were almost certainly the thing that made me feel comfortable with my tomboy lifestyle. Mel C really made me feel like girls could have interests outside of stereotypically feminine things and that was a revelation as an eight-year-old,' explains one surveyee, who spent weeks begging her parents for a pair of Adidas popper trackie bottoms, then immediately ripped a hole in the knee of them playing football. 'It's possible I was too sporty to be Sporty Spice.'

Writer and comedian Stevie Martin was another mini Mel C. 'I loved the idea of doing high kicks and being like one of the boys,' she tells me. 'I was going through a period of time where I wanted to be a tomboy, like George in *The Famous Five*.'

For some, the fandom offered a new identity in itself. Author and trans activist Juno Dawson was thirteen when the Spice Girls released 'Wannabe', and credits them for her 'true female awakening' in her memoir *The Gender Games*. She tells me, 'I remember thinking how I'd just never seen anything like them in my life. It wasn't even about the song – although it was catchy – it was just so unusual to see girls doing *anything* on television.' Mel C, she agrees, was 'really important' for gender non-conforming girls, regardless of her own sexuality. 'We hadn't really seen a girl like that on *Top of the Pops*. I think the whole attitude was an inclusive vibe. Girl power meant being unapologetically who you are.'

Not that everyone got the message, of course. 'At the time, it was assumed I was a boy, so my love for the Spice Girls really threw a spanner in the works. I got so much shit at school,' says Dawson. 'Being "out" as a Spice Girls fan accelerated my coming-out process. If I loved the Spice Girls that much, I had to be gay, right? Wrong. Of course, at the time, I had no idea that gender transition was very much an option, so I was a little stuck.'

There were still so many things we didn't know were options back then. Or at least, not if your knowledge of the world began with your parents' *Daily Telegraph*, ended with Enid Blyton, and you weren't allowed to watch *Hollyoaks* yet. But where retro fiction failed us, the Spice Girls came through. From the moment the 'Wannabe' video unveiled that multifarious line-up, from the tomboy in trackie bottoms to the sequinned Vegas showgirl with her tights still on, we were given permission to switch things up. We didn't need to be part of a tribe where everyone looked alike. The Spice Girls' strength was in their differences, both from each other and from the rest of the pop culture landscape.

Geri herself told the *Guardian* in 1997, 'Each of us wants to be her own person and, without snatching anyone else's energy, bring something creative and new and individual to the group. We're proof this is happening. When the Spice Girls first started as a unit, we respected the qualities we found in each other that we didn't have in ourselves. It was like, "Wow! That's the Spicey life vibey thing, isn't it?"'

They showed us that there were different ways for women to be, and all were equally valid. Earnings were split five ways, regardless of who'd done what, and even their sound itself was egalitarian – they never had a lead singer, and took pains to make sure the vocal parts were doled out between all the Girls in turn. In the real world, girls were still being told they could be sweet but not successful, or angry but not likeable; meanwhile, in Spice World, Baby and Scary had equal pieces of the pie.

And as well as preaching the message of the Spicey life vibey thing, the Girls backed it up with a few solid gestures of inclusivity – such as changing the lyrics on '2 Become 1' from 'boys and girls go good together' on the album track to 'love will bring us back together' for the single release. 'As a queer kid, you pick up on shit like that,' says Dawson. (It's a shame they didn't have the same kind of woke epiphany with the lyrics to 'Spice

Up Your Life'. But there's still time for a rewrite.)

Journalist Joe Stone is such a connoisseur that he wrote his dissertation on Geri Halliwell. 'The band's ethos of being yourself is very attractive to a gay audience, particularly kids who were probably starting to realize they were different at the point that the band were at their peak,' he tells me. 'I think they also spoke to a lot of young fans who hadn't yet realized they were gay. Some of my gay friends now laugh that they had bedrooms full of Spice Girls posters and dolls before it had occurred to them that they might not be straight.'

The Girls' image was so camp and theatrical that they've become part of global drag canon. You can go to a Spice Girls drag brunch in Minneapolis, a live drag re-enactment of *Spice World* in Vancouver, and in London you can ride the route from the *Spice World* film on board a bus tour hosted by Spice-alike queens.

But while the Spice vibe might have been performative, it never felt fake. Those 'collect the whole set!' characters could have seemed like such a crass gimmick – worse than the PR company I once encountered who gave all its employees nicknames based on what kind of monkey they were ('the cheeky monkey!', 'the nerdy monkey!') and forced them to use the names in their email signatures – but, according to the Girls themselves, they were just exaggerated versions of reality.

'When we first started, we were pretty bland. We felt like we had to fit into a mould,' Mel C said in a 2018 interview with the *Guardian*. 'And then we realized that we were quite different personalities, different to each other and to all the female groups in the past. We also realized there was a lot of strength in that.'

They were right. Aside from inspiring a nation of parents to make their clever cracks about 'Old Spice', those cartoon nicknames became more of a symbol of the Girls' own business savvy than of anybody forcing them into boxes. As Mel B recounted on a US chat show a few years ago, 'A lazy journalist couldn't be bothered to remember all our names so he just gave us all nicknames. And we were like, oh, OK, that kind of works!'

The lazy journalist was former *Top of the Pops* magazine editor Peter Loraine, who christened the girls by slapping pictures of their faces on to a photo of Schwartz jars on a spice rack. Nobody remembers his name now, whereas half the world quickly knew theirs. The Girls took something potentially belittling, and laughingly turned it into their greatest asset. They did this all the time; it was virtually their signature move – they were *Mean Girls*' Regina George in the vest with the nipple holes, shrugging and walking out of the locker room to worldwide adoration.

Victoria later mused that every time she feels sorry for the group's first managers, Chris and Bob Herbert, who they fled from before making it big (more on this later), 'I have to remind myself that if they'd had their way we'd all be dressed the same, and one of us would have been the lead singer. The Spice Girls were so huge precisely because we didn't do any of that.'

Even the band's name was a jokey reappropriation of blokeish industry attitudes. Originally known as 'Touch', they changed it to 'Spice' – the different flavours, the mixing pot; it was a stew, a gumbo, a jambalaya, if you will – but then added the second part after noticing they were referred to as 'those Spice girls'. Record company execs, producers, songwriters…Everywhere they went, they were called 'those Spice girls'. So they turned that haziness into something concrete, and *became* those Spice girls. The only Spice Girls.

This was Britain in the mid-nineties, a time when lad culture was so all-pervasive that the coolest thing a woman could be was a 'ladette'; just a diminutive version of a man. To sell a philosophy based entirely around the power of the girl was a pretty radical departure.

True, the Spice Girls weren't the first or the only band doing it. In the US, Salt-N-Pepa and TLC were both turning out righteous anthems, while the riot grrrl movement had been galvanizing its own feminist fandom throughout the early nineties. Bikini Kill frontwoman Kathleen Hanna published a cult zine in 1991 called *Girl Power*, which in turn lent its name to an album and single by London pop punk double act Shampoo – the latter ('might look sweet but we wanna be sour') was released in the UK only a week before 'Wannabe'. Girl power was already out there. But your average British tween wasn't exposed to much of it, or if we were it felt like something edgy and contraband; only troublemakers need apply. We were all, however, exposed to pop music. Pop music was ours. And nobody popped harder than the Spice Girls.

I have a pet theory, and it is this: the Spice Girls were misfit heroes for people who weren't cool or sullen or jaded enough to be 'proper' misfits. The Lisa Simpsons and Pepper Anns to other people's Darias, if you will. Camp, commercial, about as edgy as a satsuma, they were rowdy and rebellious but never dangerous. Loving them became a way to kick against convention without having to trade in your enthusiasm at the door – especially if you were the Baby of your group. You could be cheerful, squeaky-voiced, polite and clean, and *still* stick it to the Man! They had a disruptive message but instead of trying to be 'alternative', they wanted to be *it*. Household names, beloved by the world and its hairdresser. They didn't reject the mainstream, they worked from within to make the mainstream their own.

And in a world that tends to dismiss girl culture – it did then and it still does now – as trivial, shallow and pointless, the Spice Girls fandom reclaimed girlhood and ran with it, many years before sanitary towel advertisers thought to do the same. Their brand of girl power might have been a hand-me-down, but it fitted us perfectly. While older sisters could find their liberation in the clever irony and anarchic snarls of the riot grrrl movement, we had something more accessible and much more fun.

'It was such an innocent time, like a prelapsarian feminism that was just about being proud of being a girl and enjoying it,' remembers Hannah, who still can't do a

What would the SPICE GIRLS do?

handstand but feels OK about it now.

Two decades on, we're now the jaded older sisters and aunties. But mainstream youth culture is still big business, and youth identity even more so. There are YouTubers and Instagrammers building multi-million-pound empires from their bedrooms. Our digital footprint is our back catalogue of hits; instead of a cartoonish, one-word personality, we have a 'personal brand'. And it makes you wonder if the Spice Girls, for all their inclusivity, marked the beginning of something else too, something that has blossomed like a hothouse flower over the past twenty years. The rise of the individual.

Individualism, they tell us, is everything that's wrong with the youth of the Western world. It's selfie addiction and 'special snowflake' syndrome, and the reason nobody gives up their seat on the tube any more. It's myriad other failings hurled at our generation by the media, as they lament how uniquely precious and important we all think we are. The 'me-llennials', as a certain sect of spittle-chinned armchair critics like to describe us.

Before Gen Y, they tell us, nobody had ever thought about themselves. For centuries, they claim, mankind had been entirely selfless, and selfie-less because nobody had worked out how to turn a camera round using their arm yet. They were too busy appreciating more noble things, such as the sublimity of a mountain top, the patterns on a leaf, or the way ants work together as a team. Community was the most important thing in the world back then, as everybody worked for one and one for all. Like a band of merry Musketeers! But with harvest festival baskets, not muskets.

Then we came along – the millennials, an army of whiny, narcissistic egoists made from apathy and avocados – and ruined everything.

An inexhaustive list of things our generation has 'killed' with our pesky ways, according to the modern press, includes: soap, telephones, BHS, wine, breakfast cereal, handshakes, conversation, motorcycles, DIY, the National Lottery, sex, golf, marmalade and doorbells. Please note our grandparents killed snuff, bowler hats and the mangle industry, but nobody ever talks about that.

Above all, though, it's our damned preoccupation with ourselves that earns us the most flak. And especially (all together now!) if you're a woman. Young women, they tell us, think too much about ourselves, write too much about ourselves, take too many pictures of ourselves. We spend too much time navel-gazing and expecting the world to magically rearrange itself to meet our needs, like Belle in the Beast's castle, being fed, housed and entertained by dancing flatware. We're not just terrible, we're the *worst*.

However, if we learned anything from the Spice Girls it's how to turn negative press on its head. In the spirit of Regina George-ing right out of the locker room: so what if we are more individualistic? Maybe we are obsessed with forging new, more precise identities for ourselves. Bespoke ones that feel real and honest, rather than picked straight off the shelf. But if that's true, perhaps it's because we grew up to believe there should be a place on the stage (or the spice rack) for each of us.

Women of our generation are pushing constantly for better, broader representation in everything, from the government to the emoji keyboard. We're hard on ourselves, often too hard, but the upshot is that we no longer accept just any flimsy role the media is handing out. While our mothers had much more limited options, we fight for the right to choose who we are, and how we describe ourselves. 'I am the sole author of the dictionary that defines me,' as Zadie Smith once wrote. Maybe it's too optimistic to hope that in 2018 no journalist would try to brand Melanie B 'Scary', but we can at least rest assured there'd be a vocal wave of protest if he did.

We are a generation of women determined to be seen, and heard. And if we're not, then we create new platforms to give ourselves and our sisters and daughters that much-needed soapbox. As the saying goes, if she can see it, she can be it.

Look at the campaigns to put more women on executive boards, in public office, on banknotes and on a plinth in Parliament Square. Look at Dr Anne-Marie Imafidon, a maths prodigy and founder of Stemettes, a social enterprise to encourage more girls to study Science, Technology, Engineering and Maths (STEM) subjects.

Look at *gal-dem*, the online and print magazine launched in 2015 by Liv Little as a way to champion women and non-binary people of colour, giving underrepresented voices precious space to write, debate and have their work seen by a wider audience. 'It's no secret that the mainstream media doesn't represent or reflect us, so we are doing it for ourselves,' the site declares.

And if we're running with the baton, then the next generation is limbering up for an Olympic sprint. Thirteen-year-old Marley Dias became the youngest member of the 2018 *Forbes* '30 Under 30' list after her campaign #1000blackgirlbooks had more than 10,000 books with black girl protagonists added to US libraries. She wanted to see herself and others like her represented on those shelves, and so she made it happen.

The Spice Girls' template for individuality might look hella dated now, but the legacy lives on – not least in the 2016 remake of the 'Wannabe' video for the UN's 'Project Everyone' campaign. Featuring girls and women from India, Nigeria, South Africa, the UK, USA and Canada, it showcased a series of UN global goals around girls' education, gender equality, equal pay, child marriage and an end to violence against women. The lyrics remained the same. The jubilant, party-crashing spirit did too – only this time, the invite reached far, far wider.

And in a society that still continues to pit us against each other, every woman for herself, the Audreys vs the Marilyns vs the Kates vs the Meghans vs the Kardashians vs the Moominmammas, we're still dancing in celebration of that simple idea: that we can all be different, that there isn't only one way to be a woman. Or even five.

And that if someone knows deep down that they're a Geri, ginger or not, then that's bloody well good enough.

What would the SPICE GIRLS do?

'I had an excellent pair of turquoise and yellow foam wedge sandals from Miss Selfridge, which I wore with a pair of Lycra bellbottoms from C&A, and a yellow T-shirt with an orange slice transfer. I mean, WTF?'

OLIVIA, 33

THE SPICE GIRLS
STARTER KIT
A 1997 SHOPPING LIST

Something leopard print!

Something camouflage!

Anything with a Union Jack (see if flag still left in loft from Year Four WW2 day?)

Tattoo bracelet

Spare tattoo bracelet for when first tattoo bracelet breaks

MASSIVE SHOES

Plasters for massive blister from MASSIVE SHOES

Or massive socks for if MASSIVE SHOES turn out to be too…massive

Sequinned body with crotch poppers (failing this, swimming costume worn as a top)

Small, furry backpack

Butterfly clips

3,452 no-snag hairbands from
Claire's Accessories

Body glitter

Baby wipes for when inevitably forced to
remove body glitter

Sudocrem for allergic reaction to body glitter

Poster for bedroom ceiling (laminated,
if poss)

Upper arm bangle

Sun In

Sun Out (?)

Mood ring

Rollerball lip gloss

Hubba Bubba. Any flavour. Except
blackcurrant.

2

These boots were made for world domination

THE SPICE GIRLS AND STYLE

'**W**annabe' burst on to the scene (and it is virtually impossible to talk about the Spices' ascent to fame without using phrases like 'burst on to the scene') in the summer of 1996, which you may recall was also the summer everything turned lime green and bright orange.

Everything, but clothes especially. Lime green, orange, lime green, orange, as far as the eye could see. A trip to Tammy Girl was like walking into a box of fruit-flavoured Tic Tacs.

And in the middle of all that colour, galloping through the Midland Grand Hotel in a music-video-riot of sequins and Day-Glo Lycra, there they were – our new style icons.

They were a headache in human form. A gorgeous mishmash of colours, styles and influences, dressed up to eleven and yet proudly unpolished and rarely coordinated. In those early days they looked like a group of mates going out on a Friday night who couldn't decide on a dress code, and one of them had come straight from the gym.

Today you rarely hear anyone talk about the Spice Girls without talking about their appearance. This is partly because it's impossible to be a female celebrity without people talking about your appearance, unless you perform as an amorphous wisp of gas, but it's also because the Spice Girls' image was every bit as important to the fans as their music and their attitude. It was a package deal. The quickest way to show other people you were a Spice disciple was by yelling 'GIRL

POWERRR' at them from a moving vehicle, but the second quickest way was by looking the part.

Looking the part meant leopard print and baby pastels. It meant stretchy, flammable fabrics. It meant pound-shop scrunchies, holiday-camp henna tattoos, cribbing your mum's brick-hued Avon lip liner for a sultry 'just had a Spag Bol' pout. It meant the sugary and the sour, the scandalously mini and the comically oversized.

For me, it meant ginger.

Historically a criminally maligned hair colour, in a pre-Weasleys era you could count the ginger style icons on your fingers – Molly Ringwald, Nicole Kidman, Cilla Black, Rita Hayworth. Wilma Flintstone. The Lady of Shalott. But for a couple of years, red-headedness got a PR boost to silence even the most rampant of gingerists in the shape of Geri Halliwell. She took every stereotype about fiery temperaments and hot libidos, used them as kindling and set the world ablaze.

Meanwhile, I had hair best described as 'classroom gerbil'. So I turned to the only means at my disposal: 99p Shaders & Toners sachets from the chemist round the corner. Shade: 'Spice'. Obviously.

There's a reason my mother allowed her eight-year-old to buy Shaders & Toners, and that's because Shaders & Toners did practically nothing. They were the hair-dye equivalent of licking a red Smartie and using it as a lipstick. But I was determined, and I had a deadline looming: a Spice Girls-themed birthday party. It was crucial to my personal happiness that I looked less like a

What would the SPICE GIRLS do?

reject Hanson brother and more like Geri, my Titian hero.

Over a few weeks I stockpiled as many sachets as my pocket money and birthday money would stretch to, then spent an arduous Saturday evening lathering them up, one after the other, watching *Noel's House Party* while the colour developed, until my unspicy locks finally started to glow like a block of Red Leicester. It was slow work, and as rebellions go it was amateur league – I had parental permission, after all, and I only ruined one towel. But still, it felt stomach-flippingly bold. I was Dorothy in Oz, stepping out of the grey into glorious Technicolor. It was like cranking up the volume on my own appearance.

Beyond my bathroom, of course, things were also getting pretty loud.

One fan remembers coming home from school to find her mum had bought her 'a load of lime-green presents', which is nice confirmation that I didn't dream the Tic Tac summer. 'One of them was a pair of platform shoes – my mum wasn't into my wearing grown-up clothes at all, so it was a proper treat. Imagine a kid that age, clomping around in platforms, practising her walk on the kitchen lino.'

You don't need to imagine it if you also lived it, and have the historic ankle injuries to boot. Like a mutation of the seventies glam-rock platform with more than a hint of orthopaedic instrument, the shoes are probably the first thing most people remember about the archetypal Spice Girl wardrobe. Even Emma Bunton, when asked in a 2006 interview for the *Guardian* to close her eyes, think of the Spice Girls and describe what she saw, answered, 'I think of big bloody shoes, falling over and hurting myself a lot.'

The signature pairs worn by her, Mel B and Geri (Victoria favoured strappy stilettos, of course, while Mel C needed a trainer you could backflip in) were most often by beloved nineties label Buffalo London, and the soles seemed to get higher in direct proportion to their fame. As girl power's stock rose, we all rose with it.

Anyone who has ever worn a platform will know that they have a special power. Dainty high heels, less so. No matter how elegant the shoe, when all of your weight is pressed into the ball of your foot it tends to make you feel slow and precarious rather than capable and confident; all it takes is one public trip to leave you cursing the patriarchy for ever and wishing you had flats in your bag. But platforms are different.

For one thing, your feet are at a more natural angle, so you feel elevated rather than debilitated. And for another, you command more attention with each percussive stride. You don't totter in platforms – you thunder. You take up more space and you make more noise too. High shoes are so often dismissed as silly shoes, chosen by silly women complicit in our own oppression. But the right pair, for the right reasons, can feel like kicking that kind of judgement right in the knackers. Why wait for someone to put you on a pedestal when you can just wear two of your own?

Of course, in 1996 I didn't have this argument fine-

What would the SPICE GIRLS do?

tuned, so it tended to come out a bit more like, 'WHYYYYY CAN'T I HAVE BUFFALO BOOTS WHYYYY I HATE YOU I DIDN'T ASK TO BE BORN.' But the gist was the same. I wanted more than just the shoes, I realize now. I craved a bit of that noisy, unruly confidence for myself. Confidence would have been so useful for navigating the choppy waters of middle-school playground politics, and for doing my Year Six SATs. Wasn't confidence, more than beauty, fashion or perfection, what the Spice Girls' style was really about?

Although, let's be honest, it was also about stuff. The kit. The *accoutrements*. If we couldn't have what the Spice Girls were having, we could at least have what they were wearing. But while there's not much way to get round the shameless materialism the Fab Five inspired in us – a craving for, as Sylvia Plath had put it long before, 'the thinginess of things' – their aesthetic was still accessible. Not practical (shout-out to everyone who gamely wore those platform trainers for netball practice), but open to all who dared to have a go. And crucially, easy for us scrappy pre-teens with limited pocket money and provincial shopping resources to copy.

After all, as legend has it, Geri and her sister made that Union Jack dress out of a tea towel. A tea towel! Everyone could co-opt a tea towel. You could be Mel C in your PE kit, or Mel B in your brother's combats. Even Victoria's little Gucci dresses were easy enough to acquire as stretchy knock-offs down the market, or, if you really were posh, on a sacred pilgrimage to Morgan de Toi. My friend Becca remembers performing 'Viva Forever' at her primary school leavers' assembly wearing 'this weird cropped top that my mum had made from a big, red corduroy dress'. All you really needed to get the Spice look was courage and a bag of craft supplies.

And in lieu of real Buffalo boots (because nobody I knew in suburbia had real Buffalo boots) the girls in my class clamoured for platform trainers from Shoe Zone. They came in black faux suede or denim, with a two-inch white rubber sole and white slash along the side. If you were lucky, you could swing it, shake it, move it and just about make it before the sole came away from the rest of the shoe and you had to finish the youth club disco in your lace-frill ankle socks. It took me longer to campaign for a pair of platform trainers than they actually lasted once I got them, but they were a glorious few weeks.

Meanwhile, the chemist round the corner was good for more than just hair dye. While trips to the town centre Superdrug were still a sporadic treat, it was thrilling to know that just two minutes from my house there was all the Rimmel Coffee Shimmer lipstick and Miners body glitter I could slather on in the time it took for my mother to pick up her prescription.

I'm still obsessed with old-school chemists today; there's a rush you get from finding your war paint next to the tubes of wart freeze and tins of barley sugar that you just don't get in purpose-built beauty halls. It's about resourcefulness. You improvise and make the most of what you've got to hand. It's true of being a kid with dreams beyond their own doorstep, and it was true of being a Spice Girl too.

Of course, while the fans were elbow-deep in the fancy-dress box and loving it, the Spice Girls' look was earning the Spice Girls themselves about as much grown-up disapproval as their music. They were tacky. They were trashy. They were lurid and ridiculous. And the oldest in the book: they were too sexy.

Miles of column inches and hours of froth-mouthed tutting were dedicated to the concern that Spicemania was indoctrinating impressionable young fans into raunch culture – a hypersexual dystopia where skirts were micro, heels massive and boobs hoiked skywards at all times. Depending on who you spoke to it was either sadly misguided post-feminism, or filthy godless harlots come to corrupt us all. Either way, it was bad.

And in the case of the Spices, even those on their side couldn't help making a snide crack or two about their outfits. Simon Fuller declared years later, in his foreword to *Wannabe: How the Spice Girls Reinvented Pop Fame*, 'It was like going into battle with a crack regiment of the SAS behind me, albeit wearing short skirts, cropped tops and stack heeled boots.' And yeesh, doesn't that 'albeit' feel loaded? Intentional or not, there are centuries of hypocrisy, misogyny and policing of women's wardrobes wrapped up in that albeit.

Our wardrobes are still used as an albeit today. Every time a politician earns more comments on her shoes than her policies; every time clothes are used as a defence in a rape case; every time the *Daily Mail* publishes the words 'leggy display'; every time we're told offhand we don't 'look like' a boss/lawyer/scientist/mother/sports fan/breadwinner/expert, there it is. An excuse to dock our full quota of rights and respect. We're humans, *albeit* ones in more frivolous wrapping.

Thankfully, the Spices were having none of it. They used their wardrobes in much the same way they used their lyrics – to have fun, challenge convention and make themselves heard. 'To be a feminist in the nineties means having something to say for yourself,' Melanie C once declared. 'You can wear mascara and high heels and look like a babe and make as much of a point as if you shaved your head and burnt your bra. There's no way I'm ever burning my Wonderbra.'

In 1997 Emma told *Entertainment Weekly*, 'Just because you've got a short skirt on and a pair of tits, you can still say what you want to say. We're still very strong.' Older feminists might have rolled their eyes and thought, 'Sure, no shit' – but for little girls raised on a diet of pretty princesses and clever, scruffy tomboys, it was a revelation.

Anyway, slut-shaming aside, the whole 'the Spice Girls were too sexualized' critique doesn't entirely ring true. For one thing, the beauty of their mix 'n' match aesthetic meant that we always had options. They were the Kellogg's Variety Pack of bands, except none of them were Corn Flakes and they didn't only appear on holiday. For every performance where one or two of the Girls cavorted in a bodysuit or wore a bra as a top, there was usually another one in baggy trousers, a giant coat or a pinstripe suit (God bless you, later years Victoria). Sure, they could be as sexy as hell. But women looking sexy isn't the problem any more than little girls liking pink is the problem; we've argued through enough Halloweens by now to have settled this point. The problem is when women are told that sexy is the first thing they should be, or the only thing they can be. Sexy as the default. And the Spice Girls had no default.

Exhibit A: in the video for '2 Become 1', a song quite openly about shagging, Mel C is wearing a gilet. A *padded gilet*, and hiking boots. There were sexier outfits in the Millets catalogue. Mel B, meanwhile, has skinned Oscar the Grouch and turned him into a coat. Even in their miniskirts and boots, Emma, Geri and Victoria are all still wrapped up in outerwear substantial enough to reassure my grandmother that nobody was going to catch a chill in their kidneys. How many music videos get filmed – even now – without a woman at risk of a chill in her kidneys? I'll wait.

While there are many valid and understandable reactions to the idea of an eight-year-old in full make-up and a lamé boob tube, one thing we can say is that the Spices' look in those early days felt a world away from the contoured, filtered faces that dominate today's beauty landscape. Back then, 'pretty' was optional. 'Flawless' was a foreign concept. The Spice Girls' style was never about looking perfect – it was about expression. It was flamboyant, camp, it frequently veered into the realms of the cartoonish. For every minidress or bustier, there was usually a clodhopping boot or a horned hairdo throwing things off-kilter.

There's a brilliant behind-the-scenes clip on YouTube, of Mel B asking Andi Peters for wardrobe advice. 'Stick with the black skirt,' he says, while she hoists a leather harness over her leopard-print trousers. 'That's a bit too … [*grimacing face*].'

'I *like* looking a bit too [*grimacing face*],' she mugs back. The Spice Girls were Man Repellers long before the term 'man repeller' was a fashion concept we aspired to.

In this respect they belonged to a grand style tradition of women dressing in a way that's both fiercely feminine and a big middle finger to male approval. Look at Lady Gaga, a decade later, dancing in her pants one day and draped in a plush coat of Kermit the Frogs the next. And like Gaga, like FKA Twigs, like Sia, like Janelle Monáe, like so many in the growing sorority of stars trying to shake things up on the red carpet, the Spice Girls' look always had a sense of humour. Unapologetically playful, often downright daft. While women are taught from a tender age that beauty is a serious business – at times, let's be real, it's basically a part-time job – they made it all feel like a laugh.

While it would be years before the fashion industry gave them any kind of kudos, I stand by my belief that the Spices had fashion clout. There were retro references – Emma paid homage to mod muses such as Twiggy and Lulu, while Geri favoured the bombshells of the fifties and the glam rockers of the seventies – and there was innovation. Victoria revived the fortunes of the classic LBD. Mel B kept the 'underwear as outerwear' torch aflame and carried it safely from Madonna to Rihanna. Obviously Melanie C invented athleisurewear. I could go on.

But more importantly, Sporty, Scary, Ginger, Baby and Posh fall into that small but noble group of pop culture legends with a look so distinctive that even the ropiest fancy-dress effort will do the job. Just like anyone can slap on fake sideburns and a white jumpsuit, or a flower crown and monobrow, and become immediately recognizable as Elvis or Frida Kahlo, all it takes to instantly conjure up the memory of the Spice Girls is massive shoes, a bit of leopard print, high bunches and an open-mouthed wink. It's the stuff low-budget small-town waxwork museums thrive on – and, coincidentally, low-budget small-town girls. Like me.

If only it had stuck. After the Spice Girls, fashion became a strange soup of pube-grazing jeans, cautious jersey separates and standard issue 'Julien Macdonald at Debenhams'-type sexiness. The pop stars were either wearing assless chaps, designer tailoring or knitted twin-sets. No more tea-towel dresses for us.

And while adult women sourced their style tips from magazines, the Next Directory and Caryn Franklin on *The Clothes Show*, I got mine from my Stylefax. This was like a Funfax, if you remember those, only without the fun. The 'Get Smart!' insert contained illuminating nuggets such as, 'Never wear horizontal stripes!' and 'Avoid epaulettes if you have broad shoulders!', with traumatizing pencil sketches of different body types to illustrate the points. There I was, buying my own insecurities from WHSmith for £1.50 a pop.

A couple of years later things would get worse, when Trinny and Susannah took the nation by the norks and told us sternly what not to wear. All emphasis on the forbidden. Coupled with a landscape where every grown-up woman we knew seemed to be at the behest of Rosemary Conley and a tub of low-fat cottage cheese and pineapple, it's hardly surprising that getting dressed became about dos and don'ts and corrective devices, rather than putting clothes on for the sheer bloody love of them.

I don't know about you, but I'm only just shaking off the influence of that era now. At the age of thirty I still can't pick up a roll-neck jumper without hearing Trinny and Susannah booming, 'Third chin!', or countenance a capped sleeve without remembering their old warning that, on big arms, they looked like 'a swimming cap stretched atop a mountain of flesh.'

'Do you really want the world to see your most hideous physical defect? Hide the buggers, for goodness' sake,' they barked, beneath a picture of a sleeveless vest. This, in a book I asked for as a thirteenth birthday present. Come the millennium, the closest thing I experienced to Y2K was having the memory that fashion was fun wiped out, whoosh, beneath a crashing wave of adolescent insecurity.

I spent fifteen years after that covering my upper arms at all costs. I sweated out each summer in a series of prim cardigans and prissy cover-ups, because I thought they were the only way to make my body look acceptable. If you had a big rack or hips during the mid-noughties indie years, your prescribed uniform was 'full-skirted 1950s rockabilly rehash' and that was that, no griping. The Spice Girls years felt so liberating by comparison.

And now, in 2018? While many style bastions of our youth are no more – Bay Trading and MK One have bitten the dust, Boots Seventeen is winding down, Tammy Girl was orphaned, adopted, and then finally died when BHS did – the nineties revival has sent plenty of others galloping back again to make us feel ancient. The pastel-and-neon palette, the tattoo necklaces (flogged in Topshop for *a tenner* this time, hilarious), the dungarees and smart-casual trackie bottoms, the gleefully impractical accessories (this year I saw a teen on her way to Wireless Festival with her contraband booze in an inflatable rucksack). And the shoes, the shoes! Rihanna's Fenty x Puma collaboration served up great big marshmallows of sneakers, and Buffalo London itself sniffed a nostalgia opportunity and re-released its classic boots in 2017. A whole new generation of girls can now discover how it feels to storm through life in shoes that could kick a bin over.

Elsewhere, between Scandi minimalism, hippie maximalism and a thousand floral wrap dresses, souvenirs of Spicemania live on in our wardrobes too. Every time we pull on a pair of knee-high boots, or team a minidress with a faux-fur coat, our mouths might be saying, 'Mmm, yah, I thought it was very Stevie Nicks meets Jane Birkin …' but our brains are secretly screaming, 'BABY SPICE BABY SPICE BABY SPICE.'

In fact, I just looked down and realized I am writing this in a leopard-print dress and white platform trainers. The Spice Girls were my very first filter for fashion, and clearly that kind of thing leaves an imprint.

They were the first heroes who gave me permission to craft my own appearance, however I liked and, crucially, to have fun with it. Those heroes only come around every so often, and they're valuable. It's the reason David Bowie and Madonna inspire such devotion, and the antidote to all the slavish, manicured perfection that fills our phones today.

The pressure to look a certain way versus the desire to look a certain way is just as hard to unpick now as it was twenty years ago, and if I'm honest I'm not sure how we ever know where one ends and the other begins. But I hope we never forget the rebel pleasure of looking a bit too *grimacing face*. I'll ruin my own towels this time.

'When my sister and I shared a room, circa 1996, my dad used to always tell us a bedtime story. She and I were always in the stories doing cool things like saving the world or rescuing an abandoned litter of puppies. But our favourite one, which he had to tell us over and over, was the one where the Spice Girls were on tour but Geri and Emma (our favourites) had to drop out of the show one night because they were sick. Who would replace them? The Setten Sisters! It was the best.'

ROSE, 30

IF THE SPICE GIRLS HAD
A GROUP CHAT

Emma
<Disney gif>
<Disney gif>
<Peace sign emoji>
<Girls holding hands emoji>

Mel C
hi em

Emma
I'm nearly at the park!

Mel B
I'M JUST LEAVING NOW OK I'M ON
MY WAY I'M BASICALLY THERE

Emma
What would people like from Londis?

Geri
All you need is positivity!!!!!!!!

Mel C
and hummus

Geri
Yes please get hummus

Mel B
CAN SOMEONE DROP ME A PIN

Mel C
can't you ever just use CityMapper?

Mel B
I'M NOT FROM LONDON YOU KNOW

Emma
They've only got taramasalata or a cheese and
chive dip

Mel C
we could go and find some other

Mel B
ARR NOOOO

Mel C
take it or leave it or just don't even bother

Emma
Stop being so Capricorny.

Geri
I just believe in equality between the picnic dips, d'you know what I mean? That's all I'm saying, I just think we all deserve to spread positive vibes, yeah?

Geri
with Kettle Chips.

Emma
So is that a no, or

Mel C
The thing about you, Em, is you always come back with five milk chocolate Magnums whatever we ask for

Emma
Ha haha ha. HAR.

Geri
DID YOU KNOW that taramasalata comes from the Greek 'tarama', meaning fish roe? But it's not actually pink at all, they dye it to make it more commercially appealing. in many ways i think i really identify

Mel B
I AM NOT EATING TARAMASALATA GET ME A CHEESE STRING

Mel C
All right, all right. Don't be hasty, give it a try.

Emma
<upside-down smiley emoji>

Geri
Cuidado, cuidado, que locas chicas picantes!

Mel B
I AM TAKING THIS TO VOICE NOTES

Victoria ✓✓ *Seen*

'As a seven-year-old boy it felt like the first time being a girl was "cool". I was pretty jealous.'

RYAN, 29

3

Friendship (almost) never ends

THE SPICE GIRLS AND THE POWER OF THE GIRL GANG

B etween 1996 and 2000, my primary-school class had three girl gangs. The boys had no such formal arrangement; their friendships looked like a scattergraph while ours were a trio of pie charts.

The most popular gang was cool, tomboyish and evil by default. They liked skateboarding, combat trousers, being good at PE and holding hands with Year Five's most eligible bachelors on a casual rotation. In the grand tradition of popular gangs, they were led by a beautiful, ruthless dictator. She and I did ballet classes together, and it was made clear that if I revealed this fact to anyone at school I would be fouettéd where it hurt.

The gang at the bottom of the food chain was a raggle-taggle bunch of innocents. Happy and largely oblivious to lunchtime politics, they were united by a love of animals, animal books, animal posters, and keeping the plastic tag protectors on their Beanie Babies.

My gang was the one in the middle. We were, although it goes without saying, the best. And we modelled ourselves on the Spice Girls.

While pop music has championed many a girl group, all the way back past Bananarama and The Supremes to the Andrews Sisters, in the mid-nineties there were still limited models for this kind of structured, self-preserving female unit. We had the Pink Ladies from *Grease*, who taught us anyone could be friends with the cool kids if they just took up smoking, and *Grease 2* (same except motorbikes). There was *The Baby-Sitters Club*, with all their precocious entrepreneurial spirit ('Allow us, random eleven-year-olds, to look after your infant!'), who taught us friendship was good for more than just sleepovers. There were plenty of other books too – boarding-school books, pony books, sibling stories such as *Ballet Shoes* and *Little Women* – that gave us cherished glimpses of a cosy utopia free from boys. But the Spice Girls felt different.

They had the glamour of the *Bugsy Malone* chorus line, the disruptive force of the Suffragettes and something else: the prerogative, as Our Lady Shania would phrase it a few years later, to have a little fun. Permission to be silly. And loud. And ridiculous.

'Having a giggle has come to be seen as a proto-political act,' despaired journalist Charlotte Raven at the time, which is the kind of statement that only makes you want to laugh harder.

It's true that interviews from the Spice Girls' heyday paint a picture of five women high on their own banter. A 1997 profile in *The Face* opened with them discussing in earnest detail whether they'd ever eaten dog food (Mel C had, Mel B hadn't, Geri just the biscuits). Other articles had them chatting gaily about farts, thrush and open-air peeing, all riffing off and talking over one another at two hundred miles an hour. It was the kind of group dynamic you don't want to be stuck next to in a train carriage, but one that's exhilarating to be part of. No wonder they overtook the *Sweet Valley High* Unicorns as my personal model for ultimate gal-paldom.

And actually, probably one of the biggest surprises about adult friendships has been just how often conversation descends towards our bowels. It happens with far more regularity than heart-to-hearts about feelings. All women want to get together and talk about poo, really – and periods, and pubes, and exactly what's going on with our vaginal discharge. It's a lovely break from the buttoned-up business of being a woman, plus it's hilarious. The Spice Girls were no different. From that opening cackle on 'Wannabe' (the second most definitive laugh of the nineties, after the closing 'aha-aha-aha' on the *Byker Grove* theme), the agenda is set: we are here for a laugh, not love.

'It seemed really exciting that these cool, explosive, mouthy, gorgeous women were out there together talking about how positive it was to be a woman, when Take That, Boyzone, etc. never really made me feel anything,' says Daisy Buchanan, journalist and author of *How to Be a Grown-up*. As an eleven-year-old, seeing five wild, grown-up BFFs having fun without the context of boys felt like a radical notion. 'As a pop fan, it was thrilling to have an identity beyond who you fancied, that was more focused on who you are and what you could do.'

It's a sentiment echoed by so many of the women I've spoken to about the Spice Girls – many of whom have gone on to define themselves proudly, even professionally, as a woman's woman. Like Lauren Smeets, aka @curvy_roamer, a fashion influencer who thrives on her own sisterhood of fans and followers. 'As a young girl, these mega-powerful, utter babes absolutely taught me the strength of a female unit,' she says. 'Back

What would the SPICE GIRLS do?

then we had even less equality, and yet look at the world domination these very normal women achieved.'

The power of the girl gang was central to the Spice Girls' manifesto right from the start. Friendship > relationships. Boyfriends and girlfriends: optional. Girl *friends*: crucial.

That wasn't to say they never talked about snogging; of course they did. Few Spice Girls tracks pass the Bechdel test (I checked). But for five women singing songs about men, in most cases with lyrics directed towards men, it was remarkable how unimportant the men sounded. If they really bugged them, they'd just say goodbye. To a nine-year-old they made boys sound like bogies – a fun, slightly gross diversion, to be toyed with and eventually flicked across the room when they got boring. (Interestingly, Girls Aloud went one better in this respect. Their first two singles, 'Sound Of The Underground' and 'No Good Advice', barely mention boys at all. Nor bogies, come to think of it.)

A defiant finger-flip to male attention formed the core of the Spice Girls' message, and yet it wasn't puritanical; they were never swearing off boys, just switching priorities. By nurturing our friendships and putting our girl gang first, they told us, we'd have the self-confidence to really win at romance. Or to sack it off altogether, depending on our mood. Either way, the support of other women was the foundation on which everything else was stacked, like the cracker in a Dairylea Lunchable. On 'Love Thing' they made the point with help from Irving Berlin – God help the mister, warns Geri in her best back-of-the-school-bus squawk, that comes between she and her sisters.

It's a message that echoed through culture at the time, and still does now. 'You're the loves of her life. A guy would be lucky to come in fourth,' *Sex and The City*'s Mr Big famously told Samantha, Miranda and Charlotte, before they granted him permission to go woo Carrie back from Paris. Bridget Jones's 'urban family' followed the same supportive blueprint, as did Taylor Swift's endlessly expanding #squad a decade later. And years before Amy Poehler wrote the immortal words, 'Ovaries before brovaries. Uteruses before duderuses', the Spice Girls were teaching us just that.

And it was an especially handy philosophy if, like me, you ended up at an all-girls school.

When you've been to an all-girls school it gives you a secret quality. Other survivors can sniff you out at a hundred paces, with the same kind of bloodhound fervour we used to sniff out testosterone and Lynx Africa in the corridors any time a teacher's son, a fit builder's apprentice or a touring theatre group strayed into the vicinity. Single-sex education giveth, and it taketh away. Mine left me virtually incapable of having a normal conversation with a man until I was at least nineteen, but it gifted me friends for life. And with them the kind of resolute belief in female friendship that means you can say things like 'Friends for life!' without cringing.

People often say that single-sex environments are good for girls because they remove them from 'distractions', but that isn't it. Even aside from the turgid heteronormativity of the idea that only boys could be a distraction, never girls, that isn't it.

Because girls left to their own devices are brilliant at distractions. You cultivate a rich imaginary life, a whole archive of shared history and mythologies and in-jokes (my crew and I were so confident of our own hilarity that we wrote it all down in a notebook in case someone wanted to publish it one day). There were poems, songs and code names. A convoluted plan to one day all live together in a giant house shaped like a snail. Together we were silly. And loud. And ridiculous. We often still are. Like so many Spice Girls interviews back in the day, we can produce screaming nonsense at a rate to befuddle even the most patient of bystanders. Waiters get tipped extra, as an apology.

Of course, pack mentality isn't without issues. Research in 2011 by Rosalyn George from Goldsmiths, University of London found that the rigidity of girls' social groups could create a confusion between friendship and bullying, which at its worst can be tantamount to emotional abuse. As one grown-up fan told me, 'The teachers saw the Spice Girls as an exclusionary tactic in the playground. "No, you can't play with us because we're being the Spice Girls and there's already five of us…"' When you build a moat around your friendship and pull the drawbridge up, it can feed into the old notion that girls are crueller, more exclusionary. 'Cliquey', another word that's rarely used about men. Boys all play nicely together, they say, so why can't girls? We just can't help drawing a line in the sand; this is ours, that's yours.

But then, can you blame us?

Women crave our own spaces. In a world that's constantly getting up in our grill – politically, personally, dictating what we can do with our bodies, haranguing us on the pavement and encroaching into our leg room on trains – it's unsurprising that we tend to build communities and mark out territories wherever we find them. From the first time you drape a bedsheet over a pair of dining-room chairs and stick up a sign that says 'BOYZ NOT ALOWED', to conferences in changing rooms and nightclub toilets, or the conspiratorial comfort of a hand in yours in a doctor's waiting room, those spaces are sacred. They give us strength to go back out and occupy a little more of the world.

One night in 2011, I walked into a hot basement bar in East London. Apart from a bartender nervously turning out mojitos, it was filled entirely with women. And near-obscene quantities of cake. I had met nobody before, or at least not IRL. But gathered in that room were personalities I felt I knew intimately; people I'd laughed with, commiserated with, screamed with and descended into the realms of the surreal with, like the time we all went on an imaginary day trip to Paris. There were people who felt like old friends, but could only be recognizable with a mental Rolodex of photos smaller than a postage stamp. This was the first meeting of AWOT. The Awesome Women of Twitter.

The whole thing was the brainchild of my friend Ashley (or as I knew her then, @ashleyfryer), initially as a way to see if all the female friendships she'd spent the past couple of years cultivating on social media could translate to the real world. Happily, they did. The first meet-up was such a success that it spawned another, and another, and another – brilliant nights fuelled by sugary carbs and cheap booze and soundtracked by a communal playlist of everything a bunch of enlightened women at the beginning of this decade wanted to listen to. Beyoncé, mainly. But also Bette Midler, Dolly Parton, Candi Staton, the *Glee* soundtrack and, obviously, the Spice Girls. Leave your cool in the pile of coats by the door.

AWOT quickly grew from a friend-making exercise to a vocal feminist collective. It had a blog, because everything in 2011 had a blog, where members would write about their experiences of harassment, racism, assault and mental illness, as well as the myriad instances of everyday sexism that social media was beginning to call out at the time. It was a pivotal year to be female and angry. Caitlin Moran's *How to Be a Woman* was out, the first SlutWalks were taking place around the world, and the internet was rapidly helping us disrupt the status quo and find our people. AWOT was friendship with a shared common purpose. It was creative and political. And it was living evidence of a powerful fact: that when women assemble, brilliant things happen.

Back in 1996 we were less 'assembling' than 'going

to assembly'. But the rowdy magic of those videos – 'Wannabe', 'Who Do You Think You Are', 'Spice Up Your Life', 'Stop' – kicked the door down for something exciting. It spawned a whole packs-of-charging-women pop trope that we're still enjoying to this day. Christina and Lil' Kim's pavement dance party in 'Can't Hold Us Down', Gwen Stefani's majorettes in 'Hollaback', Taylor Swift's troupe of celebrity assassins in 'Bad Blood', Dua Lipa's pyjama-party pep talk in 'New Rules'. I'm not saying Rachel Stevens' 'Some Girls' was in the same league as Beyoncé's 'Formation', but hey, every little helps. It all led us to where we are today, in an era championing the girl group in all its incarnations.

'Support your local girl gang' is a phrase that's bounced round for decades, but right now it's everywhere – on T-shirts, posters, pencil cases, emblazoned on the back of baseball jackets like the Pink Ladies reborn. And with the reignited interest in girl gangs has come a greater respect for the woman gang too.

Social media is full of these proud affirmations of squad goals. 'These girls'. Team hen. Our ride-or-dies. Where once our girl gangs assembled in the playground, now it's via WhatsApp, email chains, or fire emojis in the comments section. And they no longer need to be physical relationships, or rooted in years of shared history – they can span continents and time zones, they can include people we've never met face to face. Our bedsheet forts have been replaced with digital support networks that we carry around with us in our pockets.

And if we're lucky, the fierceness, the silliness and the love in those spaces remains the same.

Whether they're the Spice Girls' model or a more modern mutation, mates are more important than ever. A study in 2017 by Michigan State University found that friends are increasingly important as people get older, with strong friendships being a better indicator of well-being in later life than strong family ties. Two decades on from that pioneering vision of the 'urban family', we are single for longer, dating less, settling down later, and increasingly realizing we don't have to settle at all – the Pew Research Center estimates that by the time we reach fifty, one in four of today's young adults will never have married. So it's no surprise that we're deciding to invest more energy in our platonic support networks. The good ones pay dividends.

Yet it's also true that despite all the modern ways we have to form them and cultivate them, friendships are much harder to maintain once you've left the playground behind. The big, defined squad even more so. I rarely miss school, but I do miss having that consistent cast of series regulars around me day in, day out. Adult friend-ships, you come to realize, require a lot more admin.

Once you move beyond the classroom, the lecture hall and the house-share, you have to schedule your raucous spontaneity a month in advance. Hang-outs become meet-ups become catch-ups, and only then after six weeks of batting 'I'M THE WORST', 'NO I'M THE WORST' back and forth at each other's inboxes like a game of emotional tennis. There's so much more 'How's work? How's your mum? What happened with the dry rot?' and far fewer fantasies about living together inside a giant snail (we planned to have a bedroom in each of the stalk eyes). While women are reportedly twice as good as men at maintaining long-standing friendships, that maintenance can sometimes feel like yet another unmet goal on our life to-do list.

So did the Spice Girls' giddy promise of everlasting #squadgoals set us up for failure? Were we sold an unrealistic dream?

Daisy reckons so. 'Something I think about a lot now is the way they idealized female friendship – and that friendship imploded. I was gutted when Geri left, but now it seems very real and understandable. And actually it's OK for friendship to end, or at least go through turbulence and evolve.'

Perhaps it would be better to say that friendship never ends in the philosophical sense. We could say that the legacy of a real, loving connection with some-one continues to have an impact on your life for long after the actual contact has petered out. But we could also say, eh, they were young. It was a good lyric, not a watertight promise.

Because anyone who has lived through the end of a serious friendship knows that it can be every bit as harrowing as a relationship break-up. You cry; you obsess; you rake over everything you did and said, and wonder how you could have got things so badly wrong.

And eventually you heal, but with a streak of emotional scar tissue that can flare up at the smallest trigger – a song, a perfume, a holiday snap, any little souvenir of a time when you were two parts of a whole. (I mean this quite literally in the case of summer 1998, when I came back from a Haven holiday to find my two best friends had bought a Tammy Girl friendship necklace without me. I saw those two halves of one metal heart glinting from the necks of their T-shirts, and my own heart split right down the middle to match.)

This is the reason 'Goodbye' is such a perfect post-Geri break-up track: it finishes everything 'Wannabe' started, with a few years of grown-up perspective. Together, those songs bookend the Spice Girls' glory years and map out the rise and fall of an intense female friendship. The day Geri jumped ship, our global girl squad fractured. She dropped the nation's Tammy Girl friendship necklace down the drain. Or, as one little girl solemnly intoned on *Newsround*, 'She's letting the whole world down.'

Even Geri has admitted in recent years that it was a bad move. And yet, as grown-ups, I think a lot of us get it. In fact, we probably learned a lot about the impermanence of friendship from that dark day in 1998. You can't take your girl gang for granted. As with any relationship you have to tend to it, cherish it, let it grow in new directions, and know when to prune it back like an unruly plant, or break away altogether and start anew. Like Brian Eno's famous claim that while the Velvet Underground's first album only sold 10,000 copies, 'everyone who bought it formed a band', so I'd like to think every kid who sang along to 'Wannabe' went on to hold their friendships that little bit dearer. I know I did.

And sure, the Spice Girls were a 'manufactured' girl gang. They were united by a job advert, not the cosmic forces of fate. But then most friendships emerge from a combination of luck and basic bureaucracy, when you think about it – catchment areas, uni courses, jobs, or simply stumbling into the same patch of internet.

There are a thousand arbitrary ways to form a bond with someone, but it's what you do with your awesome women of wherever (AWOW?) that counts. Whether it's assembling for a cause, presenting a united front, or just being able to stride out of each toilet mini-conference emboldened by the knowledge that there's someone to hold your hand, your handbag or your hair back for you when you need it.

'When I found out Geri had left, I opened my window and yelled "SPICE GIRLS FOR EVER" into the wind of our very quiet suburban street, before breaking down into sobs. One of the neighbours called my mum to laugh about it with her afterwards. She still tells this story to anyone I'm dating.'

EMMA, 28

11 THINGS
'ZIG-A-ZIG-AH'
MIGHT BE

An orgasm

A cigar

An orgasm then a cigar

'*Je ne sais quoi*' if pronounced by
Joey Tribbiani

A coded allusion to a romantic tryst with
Zig and Zag the puppets from *The Big
Breakfast*

Self-care!

Me trying to sound like I know about
Zinedine Zidane

Party drugs

Me trying to sound like I know about
party drugs

Every nineties gal's favourite reply when the
hairdresser asked how she wore her parting

A spice blend that goes nicely with halloumi

'Girl power wasn't about boys, it was about me and my mates. As someone who's spent a lot of time as an adult worrying what men think of me, that's quite refreshing to remember.'

HELENA, 28

4

Getting what you really, really want

THE SPICE GIRLS AND SEX

Hands up: who, to this day, still finds themselves blushing whenever '2 Become 1' comes on?

Great, you can be in my club. The first rule is that no matter how mature and important we become, all it will ever take is those majestic opening strains and Mel C's sultry first line for our cheeks to flame crimson, as though we're right back there, giggling behind our hands in the back of someone's mum's Ford Mondeo because – OMG, did you know? – they're singing about doing it.

It.

What 'it' might actually be, according to my friends, ran the whole gamut of creative interpretation, from 'very powerful kissing' to anatomical near-accuracy for those who had access to a copy of *More* magazine. But even if it was just a code we hadn't yet cracked, to hear popstars sing about 'making love' and 'getting it on' was gleefully shocking, particularly for those of us who weren't allowed a topless poster of Ryan Giggs on our bedroom ceiling. (In hindsight I'm less bothered about that now, Dad.)

One fan told me her sister was so embarrassed by the lyrics, she made up alternative ones about knitting – 'Wanna make a jumper, baby' – and sang them whenever it came on. Another found the song so excruciating that even in 2007 she couldn't sit with her parents and watch the group perform it on *Strictly Come Dancing*. 'I was nineteen. I still wanted to die of shame.'

Dying of shame whenever sex comes up is a youthful

rite of passage. It's the easier option, too – either you die of shame or, depending on your age and how liberal the attitude of your household is, other things might happen. You might be sat down and told a complicated analogy involving woodland creatures. You might be presented with an illustrated book full of cheerful naked cartoons and oblique references to 'hair' in 'new places'. (Please God, I would pray, thinking of my grandpa, don't let it be nostrils.) You might be told you could ask any questions you wanted, in a tone that begged 'please don't'.

But dying of shame was still worth it for the thrill of burgeoning adulthood that the Spice Girls' fruitier lyrics afforded us. It was intriguing but never scary. Even if we didn't know what *it* was, they were talking about something we knew we wanted to understand.

'They were just so sexy *and* fun. Most sexy women back then looked miserable, like pseudo-heroin addicts in a perfume ad. The sexiness of the Spice Girls felt fresh and real and like they owned it,' summed up one of my surveyees. While the group were owning it, though, she felt she had to hide her own feelings. 'I was aware that claiming my love for them was somehow admitting my own sexuality, which, aged twelve and in a tiny village, I was too embarrassed about.'

Sex education in schools being what it was in the nineties, this is hardly surprising. The sole concession to puberty I received in school before the age of about fourteen was one hour of dropping tampons into beakers of water (the boys, we learned afterwards, had been taught 'not to scratch their balls at the bus stop'), and my all-girls high school seemed to believe ankle-length skirts and red hats were all the contraception we needed. It's little wonder the Spice Girls' confident, clued-up sexuality felt so wild.

And if it was shocking to us kids, it was virtually satanic to some concerned parties. There's a film clip online (via YouTube account 'Counter Culture Mom', sure) called 'Spice Girls: Promoting Sex and Rebellion to Children'. Sex *and* rebellion! 'Many of the Spice Girls' fans are very young, and are learning about sexual deviancy before they've even learned their ABCs,' booms the narrator, over lyrics from 'Do It' and footage of the Spices singing to an assembled crew of primary schoolers.

It goes on. 'First notice that they are teaching the children disobedience to parents. They will not be told to "keep their legs shut", encouraging sexual promiscuity in the little boys and girls.' Well, when you put it like that...

One fan remembers performing '2 Become 1' in front of her class, aged ten, and hearing the teacher tell the teaching assistant that it was 'completely inappropriate'. 'At the time I had no idea why or what the teacher meant,' she told me. 'I BLOODY DO NOW.'

But '2 Become 1' was hardly unusual in being completely inappropriate for its core fanbase. For better or worse, for virtually as long as there have been records made and children to buy them, complete inappropriateness has been a pillar of pop's appeal. The music industry of the sixties and seventies was – as we now know only too grimly – built on the completely inappropriate.

Completely inappropriate was every kid who ever lisped along to 'Like A Virgin', imagining it was something to do with the nativity. Completely inappropriate was my whole Year Six class doing the hip-thrusting dance routine to T-Spoon's 'Sex On The Beach' at every birthday disco, while the chaperones stood around drinking Archers and making alarmed eye contact across the dance floor. If you were a parent in the late nineties trying to cushion your progeny from the corrupting forces of the outside world, then the Spice Girls, frankly, were the least of your worries.

No, what was unusual about '2 Become 1' wasn't the sexual content – it was how resoundingly right-on the sexual content was. Downright *sensible* even, especially now we know that when Baby Spice urged her lover to 'Be a little bit wiser', she didn't mean 'put on' a nice warm jumper. I'm fairly sure it's the only time there's been a condom reference in the middle of a UK Christmas number one. Not even Rage Against the Machine managed that.

The Girls themselves made no bones (sorry) about the song's message, even at the time. Whenever they were asked about its meaning, one of them would immediately reply, 'It's about safe sex.' Simple as that. No floofy euphemisms, no souls intertwining in a spiritual dimension, no 'It can be about anything you want it to be...and also it's about, like, war?' None of that. Once, after a particularly long pause, Emma added, 'And we wrote it.'

What would the SPICE GIRLS do?

But the condom line wasn't the only lyrical high point. In between all the candlelight, free spiritedness and yearning string arrangements, there's a hearteningly pragmatic, egalitarian subtext to '2 Become 1'. The lyrics are all 'let's work it out', 'if we endeavour', 'we can achieve it'. In the song, sex isn't something men do to women, nor is it a spectacle of hard work and seduction put on by girls while men sit back and enjoy the show. It's something both parties muck in and do together. Teamwork makes the dream work!

And it wasn't necessarily about men and women at all, or at least it wasn't by the time they'd gender-neutralized the lyrics that appeared on the album version (kudos, Victoria). All this and not a thong or a hip thrust in sight. Did I mention Mel C's gilet?

In her bestselling book *Girls & Sex*, Peggy Orenstein points out that there is a difference between sexualization and sexuality. 'When girls play at "sexy" before they even understand the word,' she writes, 'they learn that sex is a performance rather than a felt experience.' And while plenty of us probably did play at sexy when we played at being Spice Girls, there was little doubt that Baby, Scary, Sporty, Ginger and Posh themselves felt things. And expected to. If we thought '2 Become 1' was progressive, the album tracks on *Spice* and *Spiceworld* are an extended masterclass in randy assertiveness.

'Last Time Lover' features a whole festival of innuendo. 'Something Kinda Funny' manages to rhyme 'easy' with 'queasy' and yet still sound like a sext. In 'Naked', the song most likely to send parents diving for the buttons on the car stereo, Emma whispers sultry messages down a phone. 'Maybe I should have left it to your imagination…' And hell, Counter Culture Mom was right – 'Do It' is virtually a campaign against slut-shaming, before we even had the term to describe it. 'Keep your mouth shut, keep your legs shut/Get back in your place.'

Like all great pop lyrics, they work on multiple levels. At the time, *woosh*, over our wee young heads, but when you look back now, like a naughty Magic Eye picture after you've mastered the requisite squint, the nookie is right there. It makes all the hours I spent flipping through Judy Blume's *Forever* in the library and petitioning to watch 12-rated films seem futile. Who needed the car scene in *Titanic* when all the rudery I could have hoped for was right there in a cassette sleeve?

More broadly, the Spice Girls' lyrics cemented their philosophy when it came to dating. (Except 'dating' isn't quite the word – as we all know, dating was invented in America and only reached Britain around the same time as the mochaccino. Before then, your options were wooing someone in the pub, the pictures, the chippy or the laundrette.) But unlike the vast majority of popular music since records began, we can't say that love was often on the Spices' agenda either, unless you count love for their mums. The L-word was frequently mentioned on those first two albums, but with the exception of 'Viva Forever' it was either used as a euphemism for sex and snogging, or dismissed as a massive inconvenience.

That 'Love Thing'? They didn't want to know about it.

Instead, their best songs dealt with the much murkier, infinitely more interesting state of... let's call it 'pre-love'. Lust, flirtation, negotiation, shenanigans. Everything exciting and electric that comes beforehand. The grey area, where nothing is certain but anything could happen.

There was precious little pining; no powerless emotional torment, or playing the dorky gal who never gets the guy. Just like all other topics they decided to tackle, the Spice Girls' messaging around relationships was full of ambition. They didn't just ask to be satisfied; they demanded it. Boys were dispensable ('If you can't dance to this, you can't do nothing for me'), biddable ('You gotta slow it down, baby, just get out of my face'), and warned in no uncertain terms to keep a lid on their demands ('What part of "no" don't you understand?').

Even when the Spice Girls did permit themselves a bit of romance, it was straight down the line and briskly efficient. 'Don't be wasting my time' was practically their favourite phrase. They never needed love to complete them. When you consider that in the years that followed we sang 'You can make me whole again' along with Atomic Kitten, 'I was born to make you happy' with Britney and 'What can I do to make you love me?' with The Corrs, it only makes the Spice oeuvre seem all the more ahead of its time.

Or maybe it was just a more truthful representation of five women in their early twenties, out on the pull, figuring out who and what they wanted. 'With boys, you should be able to wheel them in, and then they're there and that's it,' Mel B tells documentary-maker Piers Cuthbertson-Smyth in the *Spice World* movie, a kind of Deliveroo-but-for-men business model that's curiously still patent pending. 'Yeah, order them like a pizza,' says Emma. 'I'll have a deep pan, six-foot, green eyes, pair of loafers and no socks,' adds Posh, whose latent impact we can probably blame for the bare-ankle epidemic that rages in Chelsea to this day.

Spice World didn't deliver dates; instead, the film serves up a buffet of reformed men. From hapless chaps to downright villains, bloke after bloke comes a cropper and learns the error of his ways through the sheer force of girl power. Elsewhere, a fifteen-year-old LeAnn Rimes was singing 'How Do I Live Without You?'. Like this, LeAnn! Like this.

In seriousness though, the Spice Girls made the whole business of relationships and sex sound so much less tortured than everyone else did, and women so much more powerful as participants. Nina from The Cardigans was a love fool. Natalie Imbruglia was cold and ashamed, lying naked on the floor. The Spice Girls were dancing round the desert with laser guns. Theirs may have been a comic book sci-fi fantasy, but it looked a hell of a lot more fun.

That's the most important thing they taught us about the whole business. That it should be fun. And, of late, fun is something that feels like it's sorely missing from sex.

For the past few years we have been knee-deep in a grey area. Not the exciting kind of grey area where anything could happen, but the kind used as an excuse when everything already has.

'Weinstein' is now an era-defining word. An adjective. We are living, they say, in a 'post-Weinstein world'. But of course, the catch is that there was never really a pre-Weinstein world. The world where powerful men exploit and abuse women and get away with it is the world we've always lived in, and our mothers and grandmothers before us. It's just that so much of the Weinsteining was hidden in plain sight. Seen but not heard; the bathrobed elephant in the room.

We're talking more about it now. Where once we giggled behind our hands at the words 'making love', the girl power generation is now getting used to talking about sex like grown-ups. It's important, we've discovered, to talk about it – not just because it helps everyone have better sex, happier sex, but because if we're not embarrassed to talk about it then nobody can buy our silence. Talking about it, whether it's anecdotal squeals over the brunch table or the choking truth of a witness statement, is the first step towards making things better. Gradually, more and more women and girls have been holding their experiences up to the light and realizing how similar they are. Together, that patchwork could smother misogyny like a fire blanket.

Still, it's hardly fun. Trudging on as we have been, through the slew of Yewtree, #MeToo and #TimesUp revelations, through yet another rape trial with an innocent verdict, through yet another daytime TV text poll that puts women's bodies up for debate as though they're in a village scarecrow competition, it can be hard to believe that things are getting better when they so often feel as if they're getting worse. But it's a process not unlike lancing a boil. Painful, grisly, yet necessary. We have to open up the wound and let all the crap pour out in order to finally start healing.

And amid the more toxic slurry, there have been nuggets to make even the luckiest women stop for a minute and say 'hmm'.

When Kristen Roupenian's short story 'Cat Person' went viral on the *New Yorker* in December 2017, it was the 'hmm' heard round the world. A 4,000-word fiction about a college student's disappointing fling with an older guy, it launched a hundred online hot takes and a thousand more chats behind bedroom curtains. Straight men who weren't outraged by it tended to be unsettled by it instead. Had *they* been Cat Person without even realizing? And if they had, should they be punished…or pitied? The story didn't identify a villain, as such, it just painted a familiar scenario – hopeful texting, awkward sex, romantic fantasy, bitter reality – and let us examine it, looking for parts we recognized ourselves in. There were plenty to find.

So too in *Babe*'s anonymous account of a woman's sexual encounter with comedian Aziz Ansari, which went viral in January 2018, and spawned endless arguments over the grey area; when it is and isn't women's responsibility to say 'no', and what is and isn't fair punishment for those who push things too far. And to fuel them, the discussion around incels (involuntary celibates) that has reared up since 2018's Toronto van attack, a mass murder apparently prompted by a man's failure to convince women to have sex with him. Where once being sexually autonomous could risk our own safety, apparently it could now put strangers' lives in danger too.

While all that's an extreme corner of a much bigger picture, there are endless everyday reasons to throw our hands up in despair and remind the world that women don't *owe* men sex, or dates, or attention, or anything at all, in fact. Even the nice men. Even the nerdy, shy, cardigan-wearing Hufflepuff men who love their mums and have read all the same books we have. We're not required to smile politely through a slurred come-on from a stranger, accept a drink we don't want or turn down an opportunity that we do, all to protect a man's feelings. What part of 'no' don't they understand? For starters, the part where we're allowed to say it.

Meanwhile, in the pop chart, completely inappropriate has never gone away. Over the past couple of decades pop music has veered dramatically from candlelight and soul for ever towards more visceral representations of pre-love. An analysis of US charts in *Evolutionary Psychology* back in 2009 concluded that 92 per cent of the year's Billboard Top Ten hits 'contained reproductive messages' (and to *think*, I turned the radio on that year).

And music videos are still a substitute sex ed teacher, even if nobody watches The Box any more.

Nicki Minaj, Ariana Grande, Iggy Azalea, Rihanna, Miley Cyrus – in recent years, all have inspired more panic over their hypersexualized images than Geri and her Trixie Firecracker thigh boots ever did. And while every so often a male-fronted hit like Robin Thicke's 2013 'Blurred Lines' will inspire a backlash (so awful, so catchy, so much guilty secret dancing), it's more often the women who get the flak. Because it's the women that are *visually* sexy, after all. It's their flesh on display while the men wear suits and jeans, it's their mock-sweat misting up the camera lens, so it's easier to blame them for corrupting the kids. Even if society taught them being sexy was their primary responsibility. Even if there's such a big gulf between 'sexy' and actually enjoying sex that women sometimes work so hard on the former they deny themselves the latter.

The number of young people having sex has actually dropped substantially since the 'Say You'll Be There' days – and yet the pressure to be outwardly sexy seems so much greater. So much more serious. So much less high-kicking.

Even as adults, the difference between 'empowering' and 'exploitative' can teeter on a knife edge. Women have the right to decide for ourselves where that boundary lies, and yet it can also be hard to know truthfully which we're feeling and when. Sometimes it looks like one but feels like the other. Sometimes it changes minute by minute, with mood and context and company, as anyone who has ever walked home in last night's bodycon will know.

But that's another idea we're tackling in the Great Boil Lancing of the Late Twenty-Tens: that our clothes can somehow give our consent.

With a 2017 report by the Fawcett Society finding 38 per cent of men and 34 per cent of women believed a female victim is wholly or in part to blame for being sexually assaulted if she goes out wearing a short skirt and gets drunk, it's an idea that can't be challenged enough. And for all the blame it gets, pop culture could just be part of the solution. A short skirt, Ray BLK reminds us on her 2017 track 'Doing Me', doesn't mean that we 'want it'. The question 'What were you wearing?' has inspired, among other things, poetry, a touring art installation by the University of Kansas, a *Teen Vogue* photo series, and manifold viral Twitter threads. Where once the Spices argued their cute outfits didn't impede their opinions, so now in our #MeToo, post-Weinstein, cyst-bursting world, the very idea of 'provocative' dressing is finally being unravelled.

So now the sex rebellion is twofold. We're fighting not to be ashamed of our sexuality, but not to be reduced to it either. We're kicking against that flagrant double standard – that when a young woman says she's been abused or coerced, people say she must have asked for it, but when she says she feels happy and empowered, they don't believe her. And along with our right to wear what we like, do what we like and say 'no' when we like, the right to actually enjoy ourselves might just be the final frontier.

The BBC announced in June 2018, off the back of a study by Public Health England, that nearly half of twenty-five- to thirty-four-year-old women say they don't have an enjoyable sex life. It's dismal. And if we're not enjoying sex then it stands to reason that there's plenty more we're not enjoying either.

Let me ask you this: how many times have you had a conversation with a friend about a potential love interest that revolves entirely around whether the other person is into them?

Have they done the right things and said the right things? Were they too available? Not available enough? Should they have been leaving two hours between texts instead of one? Or maybe two *days*? And all the while you're nodding and making sympathetic noises, resisting the urge to shake them and yell, 'BUT THIS PERSON IS AVERAGE AT BEST.' A lot, right? It happens a lot. We get so wrapped up in the whole elusive dark art of getting someone to want us that we forget to check if we actually want *them*. Likewise, long-term relationships can be all too easy to treat like platform games – levelling-up at every opportunity, house-marriage-babies-ding-ding-ding – just because it's what we're expected to do.

We ask so much of ourselves, but rarely the most obvious question: Are we having fun? Is this ideally how we want to spend our evenings and weekends, rather than say, at a pottery workshop or a sing-along screening of *Moulin Rouge*? In between all the point-scoring, politics and power play, the social pressures and the internal ones, the intricate back-and-forth of a relationship and the breathless wham-bam-thank-you-ma'am of a Tinder tryst, it's so easy to forget to notice if you're actually having a nice time. If there's one thing we deserve for all our hard work and effort, it's a bloody nice time.

After all, it's what the Spice Girls always seemed to be having, and it's what they wanted for us too. In that respect, they offered much more than just one safe-sex lyric. Even if a car full of nine-year-olds singing about candlelit shagging wasn't any parent's ideal scenario, when you stop to look back on it, they gave us some pretty powerful tools for future satisfaction.

In the simple world of their songs, at least, female enjoyment was a prerequisite – not a bonus extra. They set the bar high. They challenged people to 'handle' their love, rather than begging them to give it. They were never afraid to tell you what they wanted, what they really, really wanted. Hell, it was their opening gambit. If boys got a look-in at all, it would have to be worth their while.

And if they really bugged us? We knew exactly what to do.

'I remember being a bit blown away by "Wannabe". It just looked like friends having fun together and being dead cheeky. My best friend and I performed it to my mum, wearing pyjamas with socks stuffed down our chests.'

ROSIE, 33

HOW TO POSE LIKE A SPICE GIRL!

1. THE POINT

There are two varieties of 'Spice Girls point'. Beginner level is the index-finger point: assertive, as if to say, 'It's your turn to play for the speedboat! COME ON DOWN!' or 'I would like *that* melon, please.' The advanced level is a more languid variation: the splayed finger point with accompanying wink. This is less of a true point, more of a 'My nails aren't dry yet but I simply must ring this doorbell.' Only practised pointers like Victoria should attempt the splayed finger point with accompanying wink. Misuse can result in carpal tunnel syndrome.

2. THE KICK

Kicking was a big thing in the nineties. Like twisting was in the sixties, or standing in front of wisteria with your toes pointed slightly inwards is in 2018.

Pioneered by Sporty but practised at one time or other by all the Spices (except Posh), the classic 'Spice Girls kick' is a sassy variation on a vague martial arts theme. It can be employed as a dance move, but also simply to punctuate a good mood or fill an awkward silence. When the cat has got your tongue there's no need for dismay – just summon up a kick and then you've got a lot to say! Historical uses included the metaphorical booting in the face of: the patriarchy, the Gallagher brothers, non-specific haterz, anyone who wanted to have a patient chat about cultural appropriation.

3. THE PEACE SIGN

Were they peace signs? Were they V-for-victory signs? Were they a Tory homage to the late Winston Churchill, or just a cunning way of swearing without your parents seeing you *actually* swearing, like Ross and Monica's fist-bump on *Friends*? If we'd kept up our peace sign output into the noughties, would the Iraq war even have happened? We'll never know. But thanks to the tireless work of

Instagrammers to revive the two-finger photo pose in recent years, the peace sign might be back to save us all yet. Watch this space.

4. THE CROUCH

For as long as there have been knees and picture frames to fit a group within, crouching has been a key part of the female repertoire. It says, 'Coiled and ready to attack!' but conversely, 'Here, small dog, here, let me pat you.'

NB The impact of the power crouch is significantly diminished if the croucher has to be hoisted upright by a friend while wincing, 'Owww, my bloody KNEES.'

5. THE LUNGE

Most beloved by Geri, the 'Spicey Photo Lunge' (or 'Splunge') is a kind of sideways semi-crouch – a classic trick to buy oneself a bigger focus in the shot without the hamstring elasticity required for the full crouch. The

Splunge looks best in combat boots. It can also be accessorized with a hand on the hip or lower back, much like a cast extra in *Oliver!* with a laundry bucket on one hip, about to break into a rousing reprise of 'Oom-Pah-Pah'. If that helps you.

6. THE *RARRR*

Flex those claws! Unleash the beast within! *Rarrr* like you're trying to make your jaw click! *Rarrr* like an escaped zoo animal on the news! *Rarrr* like a tiger! Except wearing leopard print! It's fine, it's a mixed metaphor! *RARRR*.

5

Hold on to your knickers, girls

THE SPICE GIRLS
AND CONFIDENCE

Around 1996, one of my favourite and most vivid daydreams was about going on *Family Fortunes.* I knew exactly what I would wear – a red satin shirt and black bootcut trousers, with my hair artfully over one eye like Claire Danes in *My So-Called Life*. I knew which family members I would take with me, and how I would console those who didn't make the cut ('It's OK, you can have the washer-dryer!'). I would spend hours rehearsing witty chat about my hobbies and interests with which to wow Les Dennis. I would, I believed, be the *je ne sais quoi* missing from Saturday night entertainment.

The only part of the plan I hadn't given detailed consideration to was the fact that I was eight years old, and they didn't let eight-year-olds go on *Family Fortunes*. It genuinely never occurred to me that this would be an issue.

The same went for my imaginary appearances on *Stars in Their Eyes*, *The Generation Game* and, in my most deliciously delusional moments, *This Is Your Life*. To my mind, being a non-famous non-adult was no obstacle. The moment Michael Aspel appeared round the corner with his big red book, I'd be ready.

I like to think this was because I was raised on the optimism of the 1990s. New Labour! Cool Britannia! Football's coming home! Feel the fear and do it anyway! Everywhere you looked, young people were lording round like they owned the place. None of the self-conscious humility of today's pop stars; Damon Albarn had his feet up on the sofa in every interview. And while Britpop's crown princes brought their swagger to the party, the Spice Girls had a bigger ambition. To prove that while confidence is a preference for the habitual voyeur of whatever Parklife might actually be, it's also something any girl can lay claim to.

Their early chutzpah has become the stuff of pop legend. As recounted by David Sinclair in *Wannabe: How the Spice Girls Reinvented Pop Fame*, in March 1995, after nine months of working with father-and-son team Chris and Bob Herbert – who had brought the group together, homed them in a house in Maidenhead, paid them a small salary and introduced them to vocal coaches, songwriters and other industry players – the Girls decided that the relationship wasn't working.

Fatally, the Herberts had never given them a contract, because they believed the uncertainty would make the budding stars 'hungry for it'. It was a big mistake. Big. *Huge.* What it actually made the Girls was pissed off, and legally free to take off and find a better deal elsewhere. So they did.

And they did it in style; it was the kind of dramatic midnight caper that 1950s boarding-school books thrive on. They broke into the Herberts' office, nicked the master copies of all their recordings (some versions of this story have them stashing the tapes in their pants for safekeeping – the nineties were full of people putting things down their pants) and then piled into Geri's Fiat Uno with all their belongings and took off.

The erstwhile managers had scheduled a session with songwriter Eliot Kennedy for the band in Sheffield that week, but the Girls didn't know any of the details – so they drove to Sheffield, tracked Kennedy down in the phone book (the phone book!), pitched up on his doorstep and convinced him not only to work with them for free but also to let the whole group stay in his house. For a week. It's the kind of bluster *Apprentice* contestants can only dream of pulling off. The Spice Girls had Big Dick Energy in abundance, years before Twitter coined the term.

'Their naiveté was their strength – they feared nothing and challenged everything. Self-doubt was a luxury they refused to allow themselves,' summed up Simon Fuller, the man they eventually tasked with managing them.

Before Simon, the Girls' methods of finding fame were seriously raw. In the early deal days they favoured a kind of guerrilla ambush tactic nicknamed the 'Spice blitz', where they'd turn up uninvited at record company offices and perform until people paid attention. 'In their own sort of pop way, there was something quite anarchic, quite punk, in the way they physically assaulted an office,' remembers Paul Conroy, former head of Virgin Records. 'They'd turn over your desk.'

The exuberance didn't wane once they got their deal, either. In every interview, every performance, they fizzed with raucous, infectious energy. They snapped gum as they spoke, yelled over one another, needled their interviewers. It was energy that came with its own set of adjectives. Gobby. Bolshy. Brassy. Words that claim to be about behaviour but are really about background, looks, sexuality, an unspoken station the subject should not be getting above. Upper-class girls with plummy accents and pashminas, you notice, rarely get called gobby.

But ultimately the gobbiness worked in the Spice Girls' favour because their confidence won everyone over. It never felt exclusive. It wasn't the popular-kids-at-school type of confidence, eclipsing everyone else in its celebrity glow. It was confidence that spread and multiplied, loaves and fishes-style – and let everyone bask in their reflected star quality.

'Five girls in our class dubbed themselves "the Spice Girls of Year Four",' my friend Duncan recalls. 'Hysteria followed. We would chase them around the playground. One group of Year Four boys cast themselves as body-guards, keeping the masses at bay.'

The Girls would have loved that. They said it time and again in interviews: they didn't want to be worshipped, they wanted to spread the good news of girl power, give us all more confidence and recruit everyone to the gang. It was borderline evangelical. And they worked as hard at that as they did at everything else.

Their quarterly *SPICE* magazine, written and edited (at least officially) by the Spice Girls themselves, was rammed with confidence-boosters for their young readers that went way beyond the usual realms of 'Love yourself! Do a face mask!'

Issue four, for example, features a double-page spread

of 'Girl power at work', reminding girls that among the careers available to them were a spy, an MP, a bouncer, a vicar or a firefighter ('There are only 400 female fire-fighters compared with nearly 50,000 men, so get those applications flooding in, girls!'). There is advice for a girl who can't stop belching ('Better out than in!' Mel C tells Windy Throat of Throckmorton) and a 'Girl power in the news' section that covers Arundhati Roy winning the Booker Prize and MEP Emma Bonino escaping detainment by the 'ultra-sexist' Taliban. Plus a photo of Mel B on the toilet.

These efforts didn't go to waste. So many people have told me that the Spice Girls helped them beat their youthful shyness. 'I think they went some way to giving me permission to be loud and dynamic, if I wanted to be,' says author and podcaster Janina Matthewson, who now gets to be loud and dynamic for a living. 'It took years for my self-esteem to catch up with that permission, but they were definitely part of the process.'

Each Spice radiated her own type of confidence, and inspired her own set of little disciples. The introverts and peacemakers found solace in the (comparatively) laidback Sporty. Baby taught the kids with a lot of feelings that it was OK to wear their hearts on their sleeve, and still be sassy with it. Her sweet accessibility was her power, and shouldn't be underestimated.

Mel B, who'd have had just cause to reject her nickname for being frankly pretty racist, instead turned 'scariness' into something equal parts powerful and playful. As one Scary acolyte summed it up, 'She was always having a great time. She got to YELL and no one told her off about it! Amazing.'

While it hardly chimes with her smile-intolerance these days (no profile of La Beckham is complete without the assurance that she's, like, *actually* really funny), the anxious perfectionists learned from Posh that it was OK to be the butt of the joke. There's a great anecdote in David Sinclair's biography from Kim Fuller, who wrote *Spice World*, in which Victoria storms up to him on set and asks, 'You know my character in this movie, I'm just a laughing stock really, aren't I?' Fuller says yes, she is. 'OK, that's fine,' replies Victoria. 'As long as I know.'

And Geri? Geri was the megawatt fireball around which thousands orbited. So many girls had their own Geri epiphany.

'I was a cripplingly shy kid and lived in my own head a lot, so was obsessed with trying to be a Confident Person. Ginger was the most confident woman I knew. She made men nervous. She had crazy hair and made it her USP. She talked really, really loudly, she showed everyone her knickers. She just didn't give a single fuck.'

'Ginger really ignited something in me.'

'I look back and *wish* I had embraced my Geri-ness much more.'

'I feel like my Geri finally came out between 2008 and 2014. It took two trips to Ayia Napa.'

'The other day I overheard a stranger mention that their neighbour's hairdresser said Geri wasn't a kind person, and I lost my shit defending her.'

If there's a reason so many of us would – and still do – lose our shit defending Geri, it's probably because she was so willing to lose her own defending everything she cared about. Even when the results were controversial, or deeply uncool. If anything, seeing the grown-ups crowing and spluttering over her slightly clumsy hot takes just re-enforced our admiration. It felt like the same mischievous impulse that made you run around chanting 'milk, milk, lemonade' at your grandparents' golden wedding party. Ummm! The scandal! Look how she got everyone going!

In that respect, the Spice Girls had a double power. They emboldened the shy kids, but they also validated the mouthy extroverts among us.

Life is hard when you're naturally timid, but it isn't always a piece of cake when you're naturally loud and opinionated either. Having too many thoughts, and a tendency to voice them before thinking, can be a fatal combination for a girl growing up (and after she's grown up too, if I'm honest). You spend a lot of time inwardly cringing, mentally reliving social interactions, agonizing over the things you shouldn't have said and panicking that everyone thinks you're all the things a woman is not meant to be. Bossy. Overbearing. A show-off. Too *much*. But in the Spice Girls, Mel B and Geri especially, we found reassurance. Maybe the world had a use for loud, opinionated women after all.

This was confirmed in 1997 when the *Guardian* sent avant-garde American writer and feminist activist Kathy

Acker to interview the fivesome. We can all imagine what the editor thought would happen: a resounding clash of angry feminist intellect and overhyped hot air, the arty radical versus the bimbo upstarts. But they never got it. Acker loved the Girls. And what's more, she recognized that they had something to justify their confidence, something she didn't have – a massive, mainstream audience.

'The Spice Girls are having their cake and eating it,' she wrote in the resulting profile. 'They have the popularity and the popular ear that an intellectual, certainly a female intellectual, almost never has in this society, and, what's more, they have found themselves, perhaps by fluke, in the position of social and political articulation.' In other words, they'd commandeered the stage without asking for permission. Now everyone was dancing to their tune.

'How had they got this far?' asked the adults, but we knew. We could chant it! 'STRENGTH AND COURAGE IN A WONDERBRA.' It's hardly 'deeds not words', but as a confident call to arms, the spirit wasn't a million miles off.

Because girl power didn't pussyfoot around. While it might have been a simplified version of 'proper' feminism, it felt less watered-down than it did carbonated and packed with sugar. It was about wrestling female liberation out of the hands of the intelligentsia and having a go ourselves, in language that even kids understood. And it was a hands-on approach, sometimes literally. Grabbing headlines more regularly than they did passing arses, the Spice Girls' brand of empowerment might have been crude and lewd by today's standards, but as poster girls for confidence and self-esteem there was no beating them. For a highbrow audience, that bravado might have been grating. But for a young girl, it was nothing short of intoxicating.

'I think that some of my early role models being loud, funny women, who were totally unapologetic, is a legacy that will never leave me,' says one loud, funny, thirty-something fan. 'They were just unguarded and mad and brilliant,' agrees another. 'I think as women we're often so conscious of our limitations and far too self-critical, but the Spice Girls were like, "Nah, fuck it, we're great and we're going to show you." I love that confidence and refusal to be embarrassed.'

'We never claim to be perfect,' Geri told reporters backstage at the 1997 Brit Awards. 'Imperfection is a sign of individuality. Maybe there's just some girls and boys out there that feel the same as us.' There were! We did! We do!

The whole 'flawed but fearless' message meant a lot to us back then, but it means almost more now. Because two decades later, a lot of that pre-teen confidence has evaporated.

Never mind *Family Fortunes*, these days I get performance anxiety in the Post Office queue. I will take a thirty-minute detour rather than make small talk on the tube. I can't ask a question at a Q&A session for fear that nerves will overwhelm me and I will accidentally yell out 'BALLBAGS!' And I know it's not just me, because if there's one thing my peers have no qualms being forthright about, it's exactly how bad at being forthright we all are.

We know the official line: as a generation our self-esteem is at an all-time low, crippled by insecurity both emotional and material. Our generation is the anxious generation, the stressed generation and the depressed generation. We're the apologetic generation, particularly women, peppering our emails with justs and sorrys, then re-reading everything in Sent Items to be sure. And all research suggests that when it comes to confidence and contentment, the Gen Z-ers coming up behind us are in an even worse state than we are.

As a result, confidence has become the opiate of the millennial masses. Even the word has taken on a sparkly, marketable quality – like 'self-care' before it, and 'joy'. We're sold it from every angle, yet the more it's peddled, the less everybody seems to have. While social media often appears to be overflowing with the stuff – so many mirror selfies, so many strong opinions weakly held – once you scratch the surface, all anyone wants to talk about is how actually, secretly, they think they're a pile of garbage. Confidence, confidence everywhere, but not a drop to drink.

And while the world continues to reward bossy, over-bearing, show-off, mediocre white men with podiums and applause and presidencies, among the rest of us imposter syndrome is rife. It's the downfall *du jour*; the complaint you hear about all the time, like gluten sensitivity in the noughties. It's hard to take a seat at the table with a little voice in the back of our heads telling us we have no right to be there.

According to clinical psychologist Dr Jessamy Hibberd, co-author of *This Book Will Make You Confident*, 'research suggests about seventy per cent of people have felt some degree of imposter syndrome in their lives.' She tells me that while men and women both experience imposter syndrome, women are more likely to suffer. Meanwhile, Gens Y and Z, she says, feel more is expected of them than previous generations, compounding the issue. 'Due to social media, they have a heightened awareness of how they come across to others, different ways to portray themselves and that comparison and judgement is far more common.'

Now that so much of what we do and say leaves an indelible mark on the internet, it's easy to be cowed into silence by the worry you'll get it all wrong. And while there are more than a few people who need to shut up for a while (shout-out to every ten minutes of 'not really a question, more of an observation...' I have sat through and will never get back), they're rarely the people who do. It's the modern confidence conundrum: why do the people who have most of it often seem the least deserving?

Am I arguing for a kind of...*confidence communism*? No. Maybe? All I know is that I want a perfect, magical level of confidence; the sweet spot somewhere between crippling self-doubt and Katie Hopkins. After the nauseous panic, but before you become insufferable. That's what I want for all women, everywhere. To be able to run our mouths off from the rooftops if we want to, but not to feel like we'll be ignored if we don't. I want both.

Otegha Uwagba, creator of the *Women Who* collective, host of the *In Good Company* podcast and author of *Little Black Book: A Toolkit for Working Women*, has a simple answer to imposter syndrome. 'The people you work with who are crap at their jobs generally don't seem to care,' she says. 'I think if you do have that level of self-awareness, you're probably doing fine.'

Unlike most of us, in our bubbles of imaginary failure, the Spice Girls genuinely *did* have plenty of people who thought they were crap at their jobs. And they openly acknowledged it, cracking jokes about their shortcomings, without ever seeming to doubt their right to fame and success. It's true they had plenty of their own struggles behind the scenes (and in front of the scenes, as the tabloid press scavenged for stories in the later years), but for the fans there was nothing more inspiring in the world than watching them stomp their way to world domination, cackling all the way. 'There was just an absolute lack of pause or apology,' one fan reflected to me. 'That's really bucking the norm, even now.'

Everything they did screamed self-belief – the way they dressed, the way they danced, the way they spoke and sang and screamed, the career choices they made – despite none of it ever being perfect. If you wait for perfect, you never get anywhere. Or, in the immortal words of Geri Halliwell, 'I don't know what I'm doing, but I'm damn well going to do it.'

There's so much we could learn from that attitude today. That being less than flawless does not negate our right to have a voice and have a bash. That people are allowed to get it wrong, as long as they're listening and trying. That yes, we need to have thoughtful, eloquent debates and strive for betterness, but we also need the confidence to get gobby and have a go right now.

The Spice Girls knew they weren't intellectual heavyweights or natural-born opinion leaders, but they also never saw that as a reason to pipe down or hold back. They crashed on regardless. Like those six-year-olds driving a lorry.

Or perhaps more like Victoria in those five-inch heels, jumping a double decker bus across Tower Bridge. And we all know how that one ends.

What would the SPICE GIRLS do?

'Girl power meant I could be a girly girl but also play football and lunch with the boys. It made it legit to be the cleverest in my class, and the only girl on the top table in primary school.'

YAZ, 26

IF THE SPICE GIRLS DID PINTEREST

Motivational quotes to help you live your best Spicey life vibey thing…

TODAY, YOU ARE THE TRUE MEANING OF "ZIG-A-ZIG-AH".

Look for the rainbow in every storm.

Be the change you want to see in the world! Unless it's 30p for a Fantasy Ball Chupa Chup, because that really won't work.

If you can't handle me at my Mel B's rap in 'Weekend Love', you don't deserve me at my Mel B's rap in 'Wannabe'.

But first, Pepsi.

Dance like Nelson Mandela is watching.

Not all heroes wear capes. Some wear little Gucci dresses.

IT DOESN'T MATTER HOW SUCCESSFUL YOU ARE. SOMETIMES YOU STILL HAVE TO GO AND PEE IN THE WOODS.

'I still regularly look at the men I work with and think, "Who do you think you are?"'

ABI, 45

6

What's driving you is ambition (and fretting)

THE SPICE GIRLS AND SUCCESS

The year is 2012. The location: London's glamorous West End, next to Jamie's Italian and the Ugg boot emporium. The curtain has just come down on the first half of *Viva Forever!*, the Spice Girls musical the world didn't know it wanted.

In a frenzy of page-refreshing and bank details and passive-aggressive debates over theatre seating bands, we were among the thousands of erstwhile fans who'd booked tickets the minute they'd gone on sale. We'd waited for six months, in fevered anticipation. 'OMG,' we'd squeaked every time we remembered about it. 'OMG. Can't wait. Ahh.'

And now, as the lights come up and the rest of the audience start scrabbling for the toilets and ice cream, my friends sit in silence. Six of us in the front row of the Grand Circle (price band B), totally mute. I will not be the first to speak, I vow. Someone exhales. Someone else coughs, then chuckles nervously. Eventually, my flatmate Tara bites the bullet.

'I just thought they had…more songs,' she says.

'And…better songs.'

We all did, if we're honest. We buy drinks from the bar and watch the second half in a haze of gin and bewilderment. Has there been a terrible mistake? Had the Spice Girls been the Emperor's New Clothes of pop music all along? Were we nothing but naked fools now, thirty-five quid plus a £5 programme poorer?

The theatre-going public felt much the same way and *Viva Forever!* (we should have known – nothing ever lives up to the promise of a mandatory exclamation mark) had closed within seven months, at a rumoured loss of £5 million.

The press crowed, the critics smirked, the Spices tweeted how 'gutted' and 'devastated' they were. And for once the fans were largely silent, I think partly because we were trying to work out what went wrong. Only a few months earlier we'd been crying at the Olympics closing ceremony; now we were wincing at stage school kids singing the dregs of Mel C's solo back catalogue.

Still, the criticism was nothing new. You could publish a whole compendium of Bitter Things People Have Said About the Spice Girls. And then a second volume: Bitter Things Famous People Have Said About the Spice Girls. George Harrison jeered that the best thing about the Spice Girls was that 'you can watch them with the sound turned off'. Chris Evans once told them to 'Fuck back off to *Live and Kicking* where they belonged' (he later changed his mind, and dated Geri Halliwell to prove the point). Thom Yorke from Radiohead declared them – because there is nothing pretentious boys love more than a bit of hyperbole – the devil incarnate.

'I agree with whoever said the Spice Girls are soft porn; they're the Antichrist,' he whined at the end of 1997. 'I don't want any part of it, and if I had kids I wouldn't want them to have any part of it either. I'd go and live on an island where you can't get hold of any Spice Girls stuff.' Wikipedia informs me Yorke now has two children and lives in Oxfordshire.

Even those who praised the Spice Girls tended to do so begrudgingly, smirkingly, the way things beloved by girls and gay men so often are. Either they were a guilty pleasure – eyes rolling, tongue in cheek, lol-would-you-hark-at-kooky-me – or they have to be justified with a deeper intellectual value, as when people tell you it's OK to love ABBA because their production techniques were, like, so ahead of their time.

Over the years the Spices have been dissected, decried, chewed over, torn down, built back up and thoroughly analysed by the press and the public, and the verdict that tends to emerge most often goes like this: 1) The Spice Girls didn't actually have any talent, but 2) didn't they do well, considering?

'Didn't they do well, considering they had no talent?' is one of people's favourite ways to damn with faint praise. People say the same about Madonna, Kylie Minogue, Paris Hilton and the Kardashians – although unshockingly less often about, you know, men. 'Didn't Coldplay do well, considering Chris Martin has a voice like a bilious goose?' said no one, ever.

If you're a supposedly untalented woman who manages to claw her way to success, you might – at best – be granted the consolation prize: being 'a great businesswoman'.

It sounds like a compliment, but secretly it's designed to make the subject sound manipulative and fraudulent. She *bamboozled* us into supporting her talentless career with her damned tricksy *bizzness skills*! The next thing I knew I woke up and I owned every one of her albums, Your Honour!

Everyone from Dolly Parton to Katie Price has been declared 'a great businesswoman', sometimes deservedly and sometimes seemingly for little more than wearing a pinstripe blazer over a bra. And yet curiously, not the Spice Girls. When it comes to the Spice Girls, even now, the myth endures that they had basically nothing to do with their own success. Their colossal, record-breaking, establishment-quaking success.

The figures bear repeating: with 85 million record sales worldwide, they're still the best-selling female music group of all time. Still. *Spice* sold 31 million copies worldwide, making it the biggest-selling album by a girl group in history, and almost more ubiquitous in nineties homes than those dancing plastic sunflowers with sunglasses on. In a couple of years, the Spice Girls achieved more than Girls Aloud or Destiny's Child did in ten. It took two decades for another girl group (Little Mix) to break even one of their chart records. They were the first act to have their first six singles consecutively reach number one in the UK charts (no, not even the Beatles) and 'Wannabe' was the highest ever US chart debut by a British group (still no).

'Wannabe' alone has a pedigree to belie its name: the best-selling single by a girl group ever, it reached number one in thirty-seven countries and sold 7 million copies worldwide. In 1998 a *Big Breakfast* viewer asked if the Girls had a pension. 'Yeah, it's called "Wannabe",' quipped Melanie C.

And its legend lives on – in 2016 Spotify announced the song had been streamed on the service for the equivalent of 1,000 years, while a 2014 study by Manchester's Museum of Science and Industry announced it was the catchiest pop single of all time. Participants identified the song within 2.29 seconds. Nobody has ever bopped from side to side on a dance floor doing the inane, grinning, 'I'll recognize it in a minute' face to 'Wannabe', and for that reason alone we are grateful.

But their success was wrapped up in much more than earworms. 'For me, the Spice Girls were an embodiment of the all-consuming power of pop culture – a phenomenon that people are often too swift to judge,' says Alice Vincent, culture writer for the *Telegraph* and long-time Spice advocate. 'For eighteen months they were the five most powerful women in the world; they defined our news agenda and our sense of identity as a country. I genuinely believe that. They were, in terms of their fame, the female Beatles, and the fact people will scoff at that statement is because they were women. We've never seen a boy band achieve their success.'

Their achievements were all the more startling when we consider how testosterone-steeped the musical landscape was at the time. You couldn't swing a dick in an industry green room without bashing into, well, ten other dicks. Or, as Victoria noted more eloquently in the documentary *20 Years of Spice*: 'We were constantly coming up against these barriers. It was all about boys – boys sell records, boys sell videos, boys sell magazines.

And we were, like, well come on, it's time to change.'

Change it they did. In the space of a few weeks, the boys had been overthrown, the Girls were on every magazine cover and the tills kept on ringing. 'Just when boys with guitars threaten to rule pop life,' as Paul Gorman opened their very first interview, for *Music Week*, 'an all-girl, in-yer-face pop group have arrived with enough sass to burst that rockist bubble.'

But as successful women the world over know only too well, sometimes when people believe you can't do something, literally doing it in front of them still isn't enough evidence to the contrary. Yes, OK, everyone said, *but...* they're manufactured, aren't they?

In the wake of grunge, Madchester, and surly, art college indie, the 'm' word had become the worst kind of insult. To be manufactured was to be inauthentic, utterly devoid of cred, no more than a squeaky plastic chew toy for the Man. And not just the Man, but a man. Specifically, Simon Fuller. How could the Spice Girls pretend to champion girl power, people said, when we all knew a bloke was pulling the strings?

Au contraire, haters. Delve into the facts even just a little bit, and it quickly becomes clear that despite their roots in an audition room, the Spice Girls were self-made women. They were always determined to set the record straight in interviews: they'd spent a year managing themselves, working on their own material and crafting their package before they hired a new manager.

'We feel so passionately about what we do. All our

material, even coming down to what's on the front cover of an album. We make the last decision,' Victoria told a Canadian TV host proudly in 1997. And if you don't believe me or them, believe biographer David Sinclair (a man), who emphatically debunks the idea that Fuller was responsible for the group's success in his 2004 book *Wannabe: How the Spice Girls Reinvented Pop Fame*.

'Fuller may have advised, moulded, steered and organised them to take maximum advantage of their talents – just as any good manager would strive to do for any act. But there is no question of him having "invented" or manufactured the Spice Girls. After all, they gave him the job (and ultimately would take it away again) – not the other way round.'

Or pop mogul Pete Waterman, wheeled in on *60 Minutes Australia* in 1997 to confirm that yes, it was OK, the Girls *did* have a modicum of ability. 'To do what they've done, they've got to have some talent,' he declared. 'I came away from meeting these "sassy" young ladies with the opinion that they *are* a deal smarter than the image might portray,' added the programme's presenter, Richard Carleton, which was generous of him.

Talent may be subjective, but hard work is not. Interviews with the group's early collaborators paint a consistent picture of the women as tirelessly determined and tenacious, with strong views on every single detail of their careers. Barely a decision was made during their development and tenure at the top of the charts that wasn't debated, analysed and decided on by the

Girls themselves through group consensus ('It's like the knights of the round table,' Geri told one journalist in 1997). They maintained that steely nerved organizational prowess and diplomatic skill for five solid years, in more than twenty different countries. I can't co-plan a hen weekend without wanting to murder everyone. Don't tell me the Spice Girls weren't great businesswomen.

Along with their brazen, balls-out confidence, they did something a little less rock 'n' roll: they tried. Incredibly hard. They knew their audience, they believed in their product, and, like the Del Boys of showbiz, they were never squeamish about selling it out of a car boot.

While other, cooler musicians seemed to pretend success was an accident – like they'd sat down for a jam session in a garage and the next thing they knew they were at a cookout on Richard Branson's island – the Spice Girls were always unfailingly honest about how the sausage got made. Fame was part of their business model, not just a faintly awkward by-product of their art. And in that very public example of pulling oneself up by one's Buffalo laces, they blazed a trail for working-class women everywhere. With enough sheer, bloody-minded determination you could be anything you wanted.

'You could tell from the way they projected themselves that they'd had to work and graft to get there,' says culture journalist Nick Levine, who believes it's also part of the reason they became LGBTQ+ icons. 'I think when you're in the closet and working out who you are, to see someone being unapologetically themselves when there's been a bit of a struggle beforehand, that's extremely relatable.'

Let's be honest, the struggle was still going on in some of their live performances – but it never mattered to the fans. Any time they hit a bum note or fumbled a dance step, it only seemed to make us love them more. Even to-day, if you look up live performances on YouTube, there's a curious lack of venom in the comments sections. We wanted them to succeed, because it felt like a little part of us was succeeding with them.

It helped that they always seemed to relish their success so much. There's a scene in *Raw Spice*, the 2001 documentary made up of old video footage from their pre-'Wannabe' pop bootcamp days, where Geri holds forth on just how damned fortunate they all felt to be where they were – and at that point, they hadn't even got anywhere yet. 'We are SO LUCKY, do you know what I mean?' she yells with the fervour of a megaphone street preacher, while the others murmur agreement.

'We are doing EXACTLY what we want to do, we are pursuing a DREAM,' she raves. 'And I tell you what, there's millions of kids out there that want to be pop stars, d'you know what I mean, and we are actually taking that step, getting closer and closer to a dream. D'you know what I mean? And I couldn't be happier, d'you know what I mean?'

Geri, we know what you mean.

Any kid who read Noel Streatfeild books, watched *The Biz* on CBBC or spent Sunday nights singing into a bottle of Matey bubble bath for an audience of Body Shop animal soaps knows what you mean. Just like their parents did before them, and our kids will too. At a certain age, fame feels like the elixir of life. Deep down we're all just waiting for someone to come along and notice how special we are – the 'You're a wizard, Harry' moment that will transform our lives. You can be a painfully shy aspiring biochemist who can't talk to their auntie without hiding behind a curtain, and still somehow believe global stardom might be within your grasp. That it could just be one Hogwarts letter, one football scout, or one really good dance routine away.

Personally, I put all of my hope in the dance routines.

It's easy to forget now what a *thing* dance routines were in the nineties. Back then, for a pre-teen girl with even the tiniest exhibitionist streak, 'taking the stage' wasn't a metaphor – it was an actual thing you did in school assembly, or the playground. Or maybe at a younger sibling's birthday party, where relatives were held captive on garden furniture and forced to watch you improvise a five-minute contemporary ballet fusion routine to music playing only in your head. You would finish on a triumphant leap to total silence because your nans had got distracted several minutes earlier and started talking about herbaceous borders, and your mum would run out from the kitchen to applaud but you'd already flounced off in a huge strop while your dad was capturing the whole thing on a massive VHS video camera he'd borrowed from work for the weekend. Or something. Hypothetically. I dunno. You can't see the tape, I've burned it.

Anyway, sometimes it felt as though we spent half the decade choreographing, performing or otherwise embroiled in the serious business of dance routines. And unlike the frightening skill of today's tweeny-boppers (all I know is that now I fail at two types of flossing), whether we could actually dance or not was irrelevant. Just like the Spice Girls themselves, tbh.

But all that performing wasn't necessarily about craving platinum records; most of us never really wanted to be pop stars, deep down. It was about a less tangible type of success. An escape route. In my head, life felt a lot like the video for 'Stop': a dreary small town and a load of conservative locals, ready to spit-take their pints of best bitter as we, the Spice disciples, thundered into the village hall to give them a taste of the future.

Adele summed it up so perfectly on *Carpool Karaoke*: 'There were these five ordinary girls who did so well and just, like, got out. So I was, like, "I want to get out. I don't know what I want to get out of, but I want to get out."'

The Spice Girls knew what it meant to be an average girl from an average background, desperate to stamp herself on the world. Not that we necessarily recognized it at the time (it is testament to her power that Geri could, to this girl from Worthing, make Watford sound like an impossibly glamorous regional identity) but everything from their accents to their attitude tapped into a mutual understanding. They were proof, as Mel B told reporters backstage at the 1997 Brit Awards, that 'you can come from nowhere and achieve something'.

Perhaps this is why they steamrollered All Saints in terms of sales and recognition, despite being less deserving on paper. In terms of cred. No, let me finish – we've come this far. It's finally time to talk about All Saints.

Blur vs Oasis, Ali vs Foreman, Frost vs Nixon – they had nothing on the battle of khaki combats vs Technicolor cropped tops. Spice Girls vs All Saints is an underdog story for the ages.

Let's be real, there's a strong case for All Saints as the better musical offering. Theirs was a quality, complex pop sound, blending a slick R&B influence with a twang of dirty indie and a funky, pulsing bassline. Their lyrics were clever. Their voices were smooth as butter. Their look was equal parts boyish and sensuous, their hair a perpetual John Frieda advert. The whole package was, in hindsight, a treat.

But All Saints were also sad. Mooching about, feeling their feelings, forever trapped in the black hole of a boy's rejection. And all the while the Spice Girls were effervescent; backflipping on banquet tables and having a lovely time being girls. If All Saints were black coffee in an all-night diner, the Spice Girls were a cherryade Panda Pop down the youth club. Or, as a friend put it the other day, 'Spice Girls were provincial. All Saints were LDN.' And when you are a provincial kid, that's always going to speak to you.

If Gexit hadn't happened, would the group have

fizzled out anyway, or gone on to even greater things? Could they have been as respected as the Beatles, as well as quite a lot less dead? We'll never know. It is one of the great unfinished symphonies of our time. But I do know that even in two short years they taught me more about the nature of success than any formal career advice I've ever had.

Number one: don't take it for granted.

Number two: use your platform for good, not evil.

Number three: you've got to enjoy it, otherwise what's the point? 'We're just having fun!' they'd insist at every opportunity.

But also, four: don't waste time trying to make it look effortless. After all, there's work to be done.

These days, some like to claim that social media and reality TV have made a mockery of the whole idea of hard work (isn't it *appalling*, they say, that more people applied to *Love Island* than Oxbridge?! To which I always want to reply: well, *Love Island* looks fun). Yet everyone around me, in every field, seems to be busting a gut to prove them wrong. Especially the women. Just like our girl power mentors, we have grown up a generation of shameless triers.

Thanks to the Sheryl Sandbergs and Arianna Huffingtons and Oprahs of the world, female ambition is stepping further out of the shadows and catching up with our early dreams.

'If she can see it, she can be it. I want to be it for little girls whose parents aren't saving for their educations, whose friends make fun of them for wanting too much from their lives,' wrote Jessica Knoll in her viral essay for the *New York Times*, baldly titled 'I Want to Be Rich and I'm Not Sorry' (even the Spice Girls never quite admitted to that, although VB's career since tells a different story). But thanks to the enduring gender pay gap, the still-dismal figures for women in top corporate positions and the myriad little discriminations that so many of us come up against every day, we're working harder than ever to prove ourselves and make success happen. Longer hours, less sleep. More LinkedIn sycophancy. The race is still on to get out of the bottom, twenty years after those five ordinary girls fired the starting pistol.

Our parents were taught that a career meant a ladder to climb (if marriage and babies didn't put the kibosh on it first), but for Generation Y things look different. We're living in the era of the side project, the networking brunch and the self-made bedroom millionaire. And while privilege means the job market is still more a ski slope than a level playing field, increasingly it feels like it's your hustle, not your honours degree, that gets you hired. We don't sit around hoping someone will tell us we're special any more; we build our own flying motorbikes.

So effort, we're cool with. Too cool, our stress levels might say. Ambition? We're getting there. But averageness? Failure, even? We could still use a few tips in that regard. Because the hyperbolic language of millennial success doesn't leave much room for being ordinary. Superlatives are our petrol; we turn everything up to eleven. And when it comes to cheering each other on, only the biggest words will do – 'you'll be AMAZING', 'you will SMASH IT', 'you're a LITERAL CELESTIAL GODDESS'. All of which is lovely, but it doesn't half put the pressure on. Being anything less than a literal celestial goddess starts to feel like a bone-crushing fall.

'Perfection paralysis', they call it, and right now it's holding far more of us back than lack of talent or business savvy. It's the reason, as goes the famous study, that men apply for jobs when they meet 60 per cent of the criteria, while women only apply when they meet them all.

The truth – that you can turn up, do a solidly good job, get paid for it and go home – doesn't sound nearly as inspiring, but it might be the next radical idea for us to conquer. It's certainly less exhausting. It's what men have been doing for centuries. None of them are perfect either, but haven't they done well, considering?

While it's tempting to see it in binary terms – yay or nay, triumph or disaster – success isn't a clear-cut thing. It's messily made up of parts that go well, parts that go less well and parts that are just plain fine. Sometimes you're on top of the world, sometimes you're in the Woolworths bargain bin, sometimes it depends entirely on who you ask. And that's as true of the multi-platinum award-winning millionaire pop stars as it is the provincial girls doing a routine in assembly. The important thing is just to get up on the stage and see what happens. You can't please every critic, but you usually surprise yourself.

Which brings us back to that night in 2012. Their detractors felt that the *Viva Forever!* musical's flop proved what they'd always said about the Spice Girls: they were just talentless, manufactured hot air. But I think it was the opposite.

Their real magic wasn't in slick, timeless songwriting, however much you loved the music. And still love the music. It wasn't in angelic voices or dancing. It was in *them*, the five of them, as people, and the sucker-punch of spirit and attitude they brought to everything. Give those tunes to a cast full of polished musical theatre performers and, despite their perfect pitch and excellent rhythm, the whole thing deflated quicker than a gob of old Hubba Bubba.

But as we left the theatre, singing 'Stop' all the way to the tube station, butchering the dance moves in the middle of the pavement, that failure hardly seemed to matter at all.

What would the SPICE GIRLS do?

'I had a Spice Girls T-shirt that read 'Silence is golden but shouting is fun' on the back. I still wear it to dye my hair.'

KATIE, 33

HOW TO
WRESTLE
LIKE A
SPICE GIRL!

Slam your body down and wind it all around.

That's it, to be honest.

7

Five angry women

THE SPICE GIRLS AND SHOUTING BACK

Around 1997, my very favourite thing to call boys was 'pig'.

It was satisfying. Quick and emphatic. It felt good to fire it at my brother when he nicked the remote, at the boys down the park when they laughed at my yo-yo skills, and at the boys at Sunday school who wrecked my recreation of the Ascension in biscuits. Most often it was what I called Liam Bacon, my Year Five nemesis, who through a cruel twist of nominative determinism had a big, shiny pink head like a simmering ham hock.

'Pig!' I would spit back every time he said stuff that I knew was rude, but not always why. Such as asking me if the carpet matched the drapes, or if I liked David Seaman. 'Pig! Pig!' I'd snap. 'Pig!'

Sometimes it got my pencil tin defaced, or a glob of Babybel wax hurled at my head. But I never cried. 'Pig!' Looking back, I realize it never occurred to me to complain to an adult either.

'Pig! PIIIGGG!' It was all the ammunition I needed.

I'd learned the pig thing from Jessie Spano on *Saved by the Bell*, a superwoman in stonewashed denim and an idol for many a bossy, bookish girl who was never going to make the cheer squad (and not just because Britain didn't have cheer squads). Jessie was a shameless swot, a goody-two-shoes (excepting that infamous 'addiction' episode), and yet instead of being mousy with it, she was as feisty as they came. Sitcomland rewarded her with a muscle-bound boyfriend in a leotard to scold. I'd watch her ticking off A.C. Slater in a way that was part

Katharine Hepburn, part exasperated governess, and think, 'Yes, that's the way to deal with boys.'

In fact, TV in the nineties gifted us loads of these girls, these mould-breaking angry girls. See also: Angelica from *Rugrats*, *Pepper Ann*, Gretchen Grundler from *Recess*, the *Sister, Sister* twins with their chorus of 'GO HOME, ROGER.' They gave us a new model for assertiveness. Girls rule, boys drool. It rhymed, so it had to be true.

But over in the world of pop, things were more limited. Pop stars were still supposed to be pliable and inoffensive – young, female pop stars especially. The brief was to smile sweetly, answer questions with just the right level of flirty subtext (for the dads) and insist you were always having a lovely time. Yet there they were: the Spice Girls, kicking off whenever the mood took them. And just like Jessie Spano, they were comfortable getting angry with boys, even when it was deeply unfashionable to do so.

The Spices were live wires in interviews just as they were everywhere else; answering the questions they wanted to answer, not necessarily the ones they'd been asked, and launching into passionate diatribes on anything that was on their mind. Politics. Philosophy. World peace. Manta rays. They always came through with great soundbites for the media and a great show for the audience, but they were also – in the words of Carrie Fisher, who had blazed a similar trail two decades earlier – 'not as cooperative as you might want a woman to be'.

The evidence is all over YouTube, and it makes for such a good binge. Watch them call out a US TV presenter for interrupting them, a Finnish interviewer for quizzing them on their shopping habits, or Des O'Connor for not being 'a nineties man'. Witness them dressing down Dutch TV presenter Paul De Leeuw for having a character in blackface on his show. It's a cultural tradition, he shrugs. 'Time to change your culture!' they yell, miming for the cameras to cut.

Listen to them shouting down a radio host who suggested they might be in America to pull. 'Excuse me! This is about girl power, this is not about picking up guys,' Melanie B bellows into the mic. 'We don't need men to control our lives. *We* control our lives anyway.'

Enjoy the now-viral clip of them on the set of their Polaroid Spice Cam ad in 1997, heartily scolding two crew members who suggested they reveal more skin. 'Why did you ask to have a cleavage showing and a midriff showing?' demands Mel B, dressed in school uniform and a St Trinian's straw boater. 'It's every man's fantasy,' smirks one guy, while Victoria mocks his sunglasses. 'You're a chauvinistic pig,' yells Geri. (Men needn't have worried, of course. A year later, Britney's 'Baby One More Time' delivered the schoolgirl fantasy in full – and with an actual schoolgirl this time.)

Feast on Mel C goading the Gallagher brothers from the winners' podium at the 1997 Brit Awards, where the Spice Girls had won both Best Single and Best Video – the only women in either category, out of twenty nominees on lists dripping with indie machismo. The Prodigy. The Manic Street Preachers. Kula Shaker. Underworld. And

Oasis, who were probably looking back in apoplexy as Sporty Spice grabbed the mic, award in hand, whooping posse behind her.

'I just wanna say: Liam? Come and 'ave a go if you think you're hard enough!' That was a *moment*, man. Watching it now brings a tear to my eye.

'Thanks Spice Girls for giving me the courage to stand up and shout back more confidently than I used to,' wrote one young, bullied fan in a letter to *SPICE* magazine. 'Now I can give just as good as I get.'

While their rowdiness raised eyebrows (a friend's dad thought they were terrible role models 'because they argued too much and were too brash'), that fighting spirit was so appealing because it was an antidote to a message little girls are taught, almost from the get-go: 'Rise above it.' Rise above it, like a patient angel. Riiiiise above it, don't sink to their level. They're just being silly-billies; boys will be boys! Not like the sensible girls whose job it is to show them how to behave.

(Show them, but not, crucially, tell them – because that would be bossy. But even Emma, famous for being all sweetness and sunshine, wasn't afraid to use that word. 'I've got a tiny bit of an edge,' she once assured Ruby Wax. 'I'm quite bossy.')

While rising above it might keep our dresses clean and our school report impeccable, it sure gets chilly up there on the moral high ground. And however sensible and civilized 'don't get into fights' might be as life advice, it also sets us on the path to passivity. 'Rise above it' quickly becomes 'just ignore it', which becomes a lifetime of staying politely mute while your colleagues talk over you and strange men in the street make comments about your arse.

If you're not careful, rising above it can morph into being a Cool Girl.

'Cool Girl', as in the mythologized, ideal woman described in Gillian Flynn's *Gone Girl*. She's an impossible unicorn, but also a prescription for the way so many women feel they're meant to be in a heterosexual relationship. 'Cool Girls never get angry; they only smile in a chagrined, loving manner and let their men do whatever they want. Go ahead, shit on me, I don't mind, I'm the Cool Girl.'

It's a speech now enshrined in modern culture, because it so perfectly sums up a phenomenon we didn't even know we needed a name for. The summer everyone read *Gone Girl*, it felt as though a rippling wave of cheers went up as women reached that page. One by one, epiphany after epiphany. That passage didn't so much speak to us as reach out, grab us with both hands and blow a fat, wet raspberry on our foreheads.

The Cool Girl appears with regularity around stag weekends ('It's an ironic lap dance, darling!'). She emerges during Tinder dates and during banterous encounters on night buses, or when a guy makes a post-coital pizza before you've even got your tights back on and then doesn't offer you any (I've heard). She's every woman who's pretended she's incredibly chill about evening plans that start at 11 p.m. with pre-drinking in a stranger's garage. Every woman who ever dialled down her feelings and pretended to like something she didn't, or not to care about something she did, in the hope of moulding herself into the winning candidate for someone's affection.

But the Cool Girl has a nemesis, and it is righteous female anger. Thanks to the Spice Girls, we're all full of the stuff. It simmers there, constantly, just beneath the surface, pressure mounting day by day until something cracks and it eventually spews out like hot lava and ruins our icy charade. Foiled again! Not cool at all. Just another emotional woman.

Back in the nineties, we had another model for easy, breezy 'don't care' attitude – the ladette. Poster girl for a new breed of empowerment, the ladette downed pints, flashed her bum in the street, fell, giggling, into the gutter and got up to do it all again the next night. Epitomized by TV presenters such as Denise Van Outen, Zoe Ball, Sara Cox, Sarah Cawood and *The Girlie Show*, the ladettes were vilified by both sides. By the conservative press, who thought their behaviour was feminism gone 'too far', and by the liberal commentators, who thought it hadn't gone far enough.

The Spice Girls were a product of all this too, of course they were – flying a flag for lairy hussies the world over, and having a lovely time doing it. But loud though it was, at its heart, ladette culture tended to advocate a kind of chill female complicity. It told women to roll their eyes and laugh it off, or risk being unfanciable killjoys. The Spice Girls, meanwhile, taught us how to rage.

While I mostly stuck with calling boys 'pig', other juvenile rebellions were more creative.

'I had stickers of [the Girls] all over my school planner, including one of Geri in the very low-cut, red sequin dress that she wore to the Brits. Every day my form tutor would cover her cleavage with a sticker and every day I'd tear it off again,' says journalist Joe Stone. 'I'd tell my teacher that Geri's outfit was an expression of her girl power and it wasn't feminist to cover it up. They really enabled me in being a gobby little shit and I'll forever be thankful for that.'

Joe wasn't the only one. One fan, aged ten, got detention for yelling 'GIRL POWER' at an Ofsted inspector. Another remembered a (male) teacher nicknaming her 'the voice of feminism' for repeating her Spice Girls creed in every history lesson. The idea that so many nineties kids were using their bad behaviour quotient to school their teachers in women's rights almost makes you want to give the group an *ex post facto* Pride of Britain award.

As well as an increase in gobby little shits, the late nineties saw the rise of something else: action heroines. *Tomb Raider* was released in 1996, birthing Lara Croft: the gun-toting archaeologist tasked with shifting perceptions of women in gaming, and turquoise vest tops. On the big screen there was Demi Moore as a shaven-headed *GI Jane*, while on TV, *Gladiators* taught

What would the SPICE GIRLS do?

us that female strength and massive hair didn't have to be mutually exclusive. The *Mighty Morphin Power Rangers* gave us a whole two women to choose from. And then, in 1997, *Buffy the Vampire Slayer* was born. Suddenly, girls across the land weren't just karate-chopping to the 'Say You'll Be There' video, they were stabbing imaginary vampires through the heart.

Of course, it would take another couple of decades before these action women were allowed to actually *look* like they spent their days leaping off clifftops and slamming monsters where it hurt, but it was a start. Those moments helped to blast the image of the 'angry woman' as a sexless, tyrannical harpy come to ruin all the fun, and gave us a new prototype instead. The ass-kicker. Feminine and deadly. 'Our culture has embraced virtually superheroic ideals of young femininity,' wrote Susan Hopkins in her 2002 text *Girl Heroes: The New Force in Popular Culture*. Or, as Miss Piggy put it, 'Hiiii-YA.'

It's funny, the things that stay with you. There's a moment in the *Spice World* movie where Emma, dressed up as Sandy from *Grease* in a fancy-dress photoshoot montage, gets mock-groped by Danny/Mel C, and responds by slapping him across the face. It lasts about two seconds, it's jokey slapstick, and yet I remembered it for years. In that moment I saw two things: 1) what a gorgeous drag king Sporty would make, and 2) that girls, even cute ones, could fight back.

Whether violent or peaceful, anger might just be our generation's greatest untapped natural resource. As poet Audre Lord put it in a 1981 speech, 'Every woman has a well-stocked arsenal of anger potentially useful against those oppressions, personal and institutional, which brought that anger into being.' Or, as Melanie C told an interviewer eighteen years later, 'I've got this pent-up aggression inside and I want to get it out…I'm just angry about general things that people with morals are angry about.'

We can laugh, but she didn't have to say it. None of them did. While other pop stars might have been media-trained to swallow that anger, or conditioned not to feel it in the first place, the Spices' wore their feelings close to the surface – and they never apologized for them either. And it wasn't just anger on their own behalf, anger towards exes or chart rivals or paps who camped out on their doorsteps; they found time to be angry about social injustice too, in an already overstuffed schedule.

But how angry can we get? That's a question that tests the ethical framework of feminism, and one we've circled back to time and again, over centuries. Wronged wives, drowned witches, the Suffragettes, the Spice Girls. Hell hath no fury like a woman scorned. How angry *should* we get? Essays, academia, reasoned debate, rising above it, sure, sure – but when do we start throwing punches?

Bikini Kill's 1991 *Girl Power* zine offered one answer: 'Next time a bloke feels your arse, patronises you, slags off your body – generally treats you like shit – forget the moral high ground, forget he's been instilled with patriarchy and is a victim too, forget rationale and debate. Just deck the bastard.' Millicent Fawcett probably wouldn't approve. But Christabel Pankhurst might.

Today, we're even angrier. Still yelling. Still calling the rude boys pigs, although we have so many more eloquent words for it now. We have tools, too, and networks through which to channel our anger. There are the hashtags – from #EverydaySexism and #YesAllWomen to #MeToo, #TimesUp and #Repealthe8th – each one a link in a chain that connects women through shared experience and creates a public archive of testimony. There are the marches, the protests and the referenda, each drawing out more of that blistering dissatisfaction. We're beginning to have procedures and legal precedents too; places for our fury to blaze a productive pathway. Slowly, slowly, the tide is turning and it's starting to feel as though one day we might have society on our side.

Yet female anger still has a fight on its hands. Hillary Clinton's presidential campaign proved that, as do the myriad other 'nasty women' still belittled and brayed over in parliaments and boardrooms across the world. A 2015 study by psychologists from Arizona State University and the University of Illinois at Chicago put participants in a high-pressure simulation of a jury deliberation, and found that when men got angry, people were more likely to listen to them – but when women got angry, their views were more likely to be dismissed out of hand.

'Participants regarded an angry woman as more

emotional, which made them more confident in their own opinion,' the researchers concluded. 'Emotional', of course, meaning 'irrational'. 'Emotional' being shorthand for 'might period all over the floor without warning'.

So the problem isn't just allowing women to express their rage; it's convincing everyone to take it seriously when they do. Like the rational telling-off they translate into 'getting upset'. Like the 'hey, sexy' that turns, as if by magic, into 'ugly c*nt' the moment we retaliate. Or the shopping centre security guard who stood by and watched while I was catcalled on my way to the pretzel stand, then carried on watching as I was threatened and verbally abused the moment I shouted back. He told me the men had the right to free speech (but I didn't?). It was my fault, he said, for getting angry.

So when we ask 'How angry should we get?' it's not just silly self-doubt that holds us back. It's the knowledge that anger can still count against us. The risk we take, every time we lose our cool and let our fury show, is that it'll hurt us – physically, yes, and while women are still walking home at night with our keys between our knuckles, that risk will always be a reason to stay quiet – but reputationally too. Get angry and we might end up humiliated, unemployed or (oh, shit) undateable.

As journalist Laurie Penny wrote in a 2017 op-ed for *Teen Vogue*, a magazine even more empowering than *SPICE*: 'Female anger is taboo, and with good reason – if we ever spoke about it directly, in numbers too big to dismiss, one or two things might have to change.' In other words, it would disrupt too much, if the world took our anger seriously. There would be too much admin to do, correcting centuries and centuries of injustice. So instead they slap a sticker over it and call it 'crazy', 'hormonal', 'irrational'. A 'bitch'.

Although bitches, as Tina Fey reminded us in her tote bag slogan for the ages, get stuff done.

Bitches are getting stuff done all over the place right now. The internet gives us a visual tapestry of all the small stands that people are taking every day. As I write this, a Twitter thread is doing the rounds – a woman who stepped in to confront a guy harassing two young women – and I know there'll be another tomorrow, and another, and another; those little bursts of anger woven together into something big and bright that might actually make a difference. They can be a white-hot flash of fury or a measured, methodical takedown. Either way, it feels so good to know you're not just yelling into a void.

There was a time a couple of years ago when I stood on the corner of my street, waiting to cross the road, and a van full of men drove past, hollering obscenities. With no time to deliver my calm, reasoned speech on objectification and how ultimately the patriarchy hurts us all (weird how there's never any time for that speech), I reached for the next best thing – flipping them a finger. As they rounded the corner and sped away, I looked up to see another woman standing on the other side of the road, also with her middle finger up in the direction of the departing van. We caught each other's eye. It was beautiful.

So, how angry can we get? Should we rise above it, just ignore it, pick only the very biggest battles? Do we swallow our anger, shut up and play the Cool Girl for strategic purposes…or give up and let our true feelings out? It's a decision we make fresh each time, on a case-by-case basis, and sometimes we surprise ourselves with the answer.

But you know what the Spice Girls would say – let rip. *Lemonade*-era Beyoncé would hand you a baseball bat. Jessie Spano would lend you her caffeine pills. And my angry little nine-year-old self would be there too, cheering you on from the sidelines. Silence is golden, but shouting is fun. Maybe even fundamental.

By the way, I was halfway through my twenties before the penny finally dropped on the David Seaman thing. To be fair to Liam Bacon, it was quite sophisticated wordplay for a nine-year-old.

11 THINGS WE LEARNED FROM THE SPICE GIRLS

Most of the 'conversational Spanish' now listed on our CV. *¿Hasta mañana, si?*

'Compromisation'.

It is dangerous to store moisturizing cream in the refrigerator, as it can be mistaken for mayonnaise.

When you win an award, everyone gets a turn at the mic.

Leopard print is a neutral.

Athleisurewear is a legitimate option in any and all dress code situations.

But you can still hula hoop in sharp tailoring.

'Kicks and giggles' is a good enough reason to do anything.

Always be nice to aliens. They might be your biggest fans in disguise.

When you make your fortune, the first thing you do is buy your mum a house.

Always read the care label. Because THIS DRESS IS DRY CLEAN ONLY, MELANIE.

'I had everything. I had two T-shirts, and enough photos to cover all my walls. I had official books and scrapbooks and magazines and Spice Girls shoes. I had the body spray, and the hair clips, and the socks. I was a walking merchandise stall. It made Christmas really easy for my family.'

SCARLETT, 31

8

Impulse purchases

THE SPICE GIRLS AND SELLING OUT

B y June 1997, just a year into their fame, the Spice Girls had reportedly applied for more than 100 trademarks. Those ladies loved a product. Which was great for the fans, as we loved anything with their faces on it. Or their name, or just a tenuous association; if they'd worn it, held it, touched it, remotely thought about it, that was good enough for us. Perhaps more than any pop phenomenon before them, being a Spice Girls fan went way beyond the music – it was about the *stuff*.

There was the Polaroid Spice Cam. 'Mel B says it's great because you can take rude photos without the chemist seeing!' I told my mum, somehow imagining this would sway her. There was the Impulse body spray. Close your eyes and you can probably still smell that intoxicating blend of vanilla, tangerine, musk, lavender, jasmine and red pepper, like the world's worst *Ready Steady Cook* ingredients bag. There were the Spice Girls dolls, the Spice Girls annuals and the five *Spice World* limited edition VHS tins with a different cover for each Spice. Not forgetting the bomber jacket, the backpack, the calendar, the watch, the official shoes, the lunchbox, the flask, the pencil case, the mug, the clock, the money box, the wallet, the duvet cover, the plastic phone with five pre-recorded Spicey greetings ('Hello, this is Emma!'), the birthday cake, the Easter egg, the Asda Christmas biscuit selection, the Walkers crisps, the Chupa Chups and a Pepsi to wash it all down.

'We want to be as famous as Persil Automatic,' Victoria memorably told Simon Fuller when the group was starting out. It's a statement fantastically at odds with the old idea that artistic integrity means you have to be starving in a garret, or at the very least railing against the Man at all times. The Spice Girls' unapologetic pursuit of fame makes them more like Andy Warhol's true heirs. Not that anyone gave them credit for that at the time, obviously.

But as they crept beyond the traditional spheres of pop fandom into our kitchen cupboards and bathroom cabinets, they became household names and faces in exactly the way Victoria had wanted. And while the cynics gagged at the shameless materialism of it all, it was a gift for the fans. Everybody could have a little piece of the Spice empire.

On the one hand, with an endless stream of new products to fill up shopping baskets and Christmas lists, the fandom could have been a nightmare for all but the richest of families. Yet like everything the group did, the bottom line was accessibility. If there wasn't spare cash for a Polaroid camera, a doll or a tour ticket, there might be enough for a packet of crisps or a copy of *SPICE* magazine.

Of all the goods they turned out to satisfy our youthful thirst, the very best were the official photo cards. And by 'the very best', what I mean is I owned some. Along with my knock-off platforms and a T-shirt my nana had bought down the market – green, featuring an iron-on photo and lettering that might have read 'Splice Grils!' – my photo collection was my pride and joy. I tended to it with more love and devotion than a whole tank of Sea-Monkeys. The headrush of opening a new packet and glimpsing a Spice's printed-on 'signature' was, I was sure, exactly how Charlie Bucket must have felt finding his golden ticket.

The photo cards were the brainchild of James Freedman, CEO of marketing agency Zone, which at the time was producing the Manchester United fan magazine. Having been hired to create the Spice Girls' first official book, *Girl Power*, Freedman was sent bundles of snapshots of the girls to include. He spotted an opportunity. 'I was like, "Wow, these are amazing – kids would love to have these kinds of Polaroids on their wall,"' he tells me. And he knew where to sell them. 'These were in the days, pre-internet, when the newsagent or the supermarket were where kids went and spent their pocket money.'

Just like the chemist round the corner, the newsagent up the road and the Saturday supermarket Big Shop were both magical consumer gateways to the average nineties child; places you could access *stuff* when scant other avenues were available. They held the promise of going round with your dad to fetch the papers and coming out with loot: *Shout* magazine, penny sweets, maybe a Puppy in My Pocket or a glittery Pringles pop box if you were really lucky. But most thrillingly, for 99p, your own little packet of the Spice Girls fandom. By September 1997, our collective pocket money had bought 25 million photos worldwide.

It was such a simple, genius idea. The photos capitalized on the same grand tradition as football stickers, but they felt like something cooler. They looked like real photos, the kind you could have taken yourself on a disposable camera if the Spice Girls were your mates – especially handy if you were that one kid in every school who went round telling everyone their neighbour's cousin could get them backstage at the *Smash Hits* Poll Winners Party.

There were glamorous shots from videos and photoshoots, yes, but the biggest appeal was in the behind-the-scenes sneak peeks. Sound checks and rehearsals and days at the seaside; Emma blowing a bubblegum bubble; Mel C doing a handstand; Mel B with her glasses on; Victoria getting her hair done in a pair of holey socks; Geri being held aloft by Hunter from *Gladiators*. Some were grainy, some featured open-mouthed gurning; today, they'd be strictly Insta Stories, not grid-worthy. But obviously that was the point.

'It was Instagram, pre-Instagram, if you like,' says Freedman. 'The Girls were very good at seeming accessible, like they could be living next door, or friends of friends. They didn't put themselves on a big pedestal – and that's why I think they were so attractive to the young kids.'

For Scarlett, a Spice Girls fan growing up in Auckland, that girls-next-door appeal was strong enough to span oceans. 'It was the first time I knew true obsession. I couldn't listen enough, or own enough, or look at them enough,' she says. 'But they were never going to come to New Zealand, and so that distance made them gods. I couldn't really believe that they were tangible.'

Merch, though? Merch is tangible. When you can't meet your heroes, see them or be them, Scarlett quickly discovered, it's the best way to harness a bit of their power by proxy. 'At school we did an experiment where we were all given a certain amount of fake money, and tasked with increasing it. People brought in baked goods or sold massages, things like that. I printed off a pile of Spice Girls photos, and they had to end the experiment early because I bankrupted most of the class. So I guess they taught me about economic power?'

Like all the best crazes, from Pogs and Pokémon cards to fidget spinners, those photos quickly became social currency in the capitalist system of the playground. You could buy friendship, affection, popularity and love, all with a flash of your *Baywatch* Baby Spice. One girl in my class, lucky owner of a spare Victoria-smiling-in-PVC-catsuit, enjoyed a full week being showered in bribery Wagon Wheels and scented gel pens before announcing who she was going to swap with.

(Her cousin. Her mum made her.)

As we bought into their endless endorsements and sponsorship deals, the Spice Girls became more powerful too. Suddenly they weren't just a band; they were a brand. In only a few months they made the transition from noun to verb and adjective; a Spice Girl wasn't just something you listened to – it was something you could be.

Journalist Chris Heath pronounced in March 1997's

issue of *The Face* that the name 'Spice Girls' had become shorthand for 'any kind of trashiness, or any kind of independence, or any kind of wink-wink-guys sexuality, or any kind of gang-flavoured jubilation, or even simply as a metaphor for unfettered popularity itself'.

'Unfettered popularity' or, as we'd call it now: basic.

I love the word 'basic', although I know I'm not meant to, because it just does such a neat job of summing up such a bitchy, hard-to-explain feeling (and I don't know about you but I am full of bitchy, hard-to-explain feelings). 'Basic', the word that crushes popularity under a cynical thumb. In a way, the Spice Girls were the original Michael Kors handbags and bottomless Prosecco brunches – by being so commercially appealing, they were always ripe for snobbery and critique.

Because let's not forget that if something is loved in vast numbers by women, particularly young women, it must be inherently crap.

Anyway, naturally there was a backlash against the Spice hype machine, and not just from cash-strapped parents. The shameless commercialism confirmed for their critics, just in case there had been any doubt, that the Spice Girls were definitely *not* rock 'n' roll. What rock 'n' roll meant by then was debatable, but everyone could agree it wasn't Emma Bunton trilling, 'A free lottery syndicate card!' with all the enthusiasm the Sex Pistols once reserved for swearing on Bill Grundy's sofa. To borrow from the *Spice World* script, we knew it would be tacky – but this was *tacky*.

The Spice Girls themselves had mixed feelings about their relentless publicity drive, but they were self-aware and always the first to joke about it. There's an interview with Jamie Theakston from *The O-Zone* in which, having been more or less tortured by the group throughout, he asks if they are at risk of 'becoming overexposed'. 'Do you mean, "Are we selling out?"' demands Victoria (Easy V doesn't come for free, she's a real laydee, we know this). Before Theakston can reply, she yells 'YES.'

But were they really selling out, as opposed to just selling owt? To sell out, you have to have certain principles to contravene – like when Johnny Rotten did that advert for Country Life butter. The Spice Girls were never ashamed to sell themselves, but then they hardly claimed to be Marxist role models to begin with. As we've already established, their principles were based on friendship, ambition, fun, personal freedom, massive shoes and teaching girls to stick up for themselves. No part of that said they couldn't make a buck while they were at it.

In some ways it was the American Dream, gate-crashing Cool Britannia's party. Geri claimed in an early interview for Fox that the group had 'a very American philosophy', and they weren't the only ones. We all loved America back then. If us nineties kids worshipped bold bubblegum consumerism, then the USA was the Promised Land – home of Disney World, Nickelodeon, Bonne Bell Lip Smackers, massive coffee cups, Big Red chewing gum, cheerleaders and the Fresh Prince of wherever Bel-Air might be. I was so besotted with the idea of a stateside identity that when someone told me Americans held their forks in their right hand and their knives in their left hand, I promptly switched mine round in tribute. I still hold them that way now.

But the Spice Girls' pride in selling out was also in keeping with the new feminist dictum that said women were entitled to use whatever they had at their disposal to make a dime – be it stripping off for *Playboy*, or slapping their face on a crisp packet. Men had exploited women for centuries, this philosophy said, therefore wasn't it about time we went out and got our dues? On that basis, by pricing up their own image and making a bundle off it, you could argue the Spice Girls weren't working for the Man so much as giving themselves, The Women, a promotion.

It's an issue we still bicker over today. Just how shameless are we allowed to be when it comes to selling ourselves? Not just our bodies, although that's a whole debate in itself, but our work, our hobbies, our image, or (I'm sorry) our 'personal brand'? When we package ourselves as a product for consumption, are we being great businesswomen – or just objectifying ourselves before anyone else does it for us?

We're supposed to *have* money, that much we know. We need it to fund the extortionate personal upkeep of womanhood – our skincare and haircuts – nice homes, posh food and fancy holidays. Yet we're still not supposed to admit to *wanting* it. We can talk about so much we never used to, but discussing money remains a taboo. Tell the whole brunch table about your IBS, sure, but discussing your salary? Yeesh. Awkward.

Meanwhile, now we're living in the Age of the Influencer, everyone's an unpaid marketing genius. People trumpet their engagements and promotions with all the fanfare of a media press release – 'I am thrilled to announce!' – and even sensible, solid professionals, such as dentists and social workers, have been known to succumb to the promise of the handbag-spill photo. Your 234 followers were clamouring to know which moisturizer you use again? Sure.

But many of us feel squicky about such public broadcasting too. We're the generation that coined the term #humblebrag, and turned watching people humiliate themselves on telly into a national pastime. You may Instagram your lunch, sure, but not without loudly berating yourself for being SUCH A DICK first. Self-publicity is a game most of us play to a lesser or greater extent, but no one's quite sure of the rules. For example, I have never felt more ashamed of myself than the day I secretly applied for a verified blue tick on Twitter – apart from the day I didn't get one.

Still, we've become comfortable enough with selling out to make it a legitimate career path. And you don't need a degree, or a Svengali to sell your wares – you can do it on your own, with a smartphone. You've probably heard the stats: one-third of six- to seventeen-year-olds want to be YouTubers when they grow up, one-fifth want

What would the SPICE GIRLS do?

to be professional bloggers. We can roll our eyes, but it's interesting to note that nine out of the ten highest-earning influencers in 2017 were female. So maybe these new DIY digital careers actually offer women a new kind of autonomy. Maybe they're a way around a system that's still so stacked against us. Which is, in a way, quite girl power.

Top influencers can reportedly rake in more than £13,000 for a single sponsored post. Though, as anyone who's watched a tear-streaked vlog will know, it ain't always easily earned. With traditional TV viewing in decline, advertisers have had to get sneakier with the way they market their products – hence the rise in 'native' advertising, in product placement and in ads popping up in the places our friends used to be. And as a result, we're more suspicious of being sold to, quick to rake people over the coals for flogging the wrong product, and 'authenticity' has become the most valuable commodity of all. Audiences expect our social media stars to be 100 per cent honest and upfront, all the time, and yet also never put a foot wrong.

In so many ways, marketing has come on in leaps and bounds since the nineties. Generally speaking, it's more thoughtful, more inclusive and trying harder to be socially responsible, even when the results are guaranteed to be torn apart in any comments section. Yet the methods somehow feel more sinister, and the mis-steps, when they happen, more calamitous.

The Spice Girls' merch machine might have paved

the way for a generation of self-made social-media millionaires, but at least they sold us Chupa Chups, not appetite-suppressant lollipops. Watching Kendall Jenner spoof a Black Lives Matter march in her tone-deaf 2017 Pepsi campaign was enough to make you wish we were still collecting ring pulls for the 'Step To Me' CD. Even if it was just a reject song repackaged as an 'exclusive' (nice hustle, lads).

And while the planet might not thank the Spice Girls for the volume of plastic detritus destined for landfill, all that *stuff* leaves behind a pretty comprehensive archive. Anthropologists will be able to study the group and its impact for centuries to come. You can picture them now, carefully brushing the dirt off a *Spiceworld* trigonometry set, trying to fathom everything it would have meant to its original owner. I wonder if they'll ever truly know.

Meanwhile, the Legacy of the Tat is already up and swinging. In summer 2018 a new exhibition opened, SpiceUp London, showcasing thousands of items of Spice Girls memorabilia and hundreds of the group's stage costumes – including a 3,300-strong collection of pieces amassed over the years by superfan Alan Smith-Allison, at a personal cost of more than £100,000. 'I have been skint for decades,' he says.

Live action nostalgia is a hot ticket right now (see also: FriendsFest, the touring *Friends* experience that lets you sit on the Central Perk sofa), but the SpiceUp exhibition feels like more than just a trip down memory lane. It's a catalogue of our collective obsession. A tribute to the sheer force of the fandom, and how far we would go for it. Smith-Allison hopes it will reel in a new generation of fans – and possibly even a visit from an actual Spice or two. It's the least they can do, really. After all, they're living in the houses our pocket money built.

Some might say it's really a testament to clever marketing, perhaps to Simon Fuller's genius more than anything else. Zone's James Freedman, who spent 1997 in the midst of the 'mad' Spice whirlwind, thinks it was a bit of both. '[Simon] was great at the package. He got lots of great people involved, great photographers, great writers, he understood the publicity…but you know, he couldn't have taken any five girls from the street and turned them into those global stars. They definitely had something magic about them.'

Magic is the word. While some people are more prone than others, fandoms as intense as Spicemania usually only come along once or twice in a lifetime. 'I wish I could get that infatuated with something again,' sighs Scarlett the Kiwi playground photo dealer. 'It would be nice to idolize something with that kind of blind passion again.'

Wouldn't it just? I used to laugh at those tabloid articles about people who spend their life savings on royal wedding mugs, tattoo their back with pictures of Elton John or decorate their house like a Christmas grotto all year round. But now I just think it must be kind of nice to love something so much, with such unfettered glee. So fully that you want to wear it on your sleeve, engulf yourself in its fumes, sleep under it, eat it, drink it and live in it all day long.

I wonder what the modern adult equivalent of a Spice Girls fan collection is. Ceramics? Houseplants? Promotional canvas tote bags? Maybe it's our slogan sweatshirts and perspex word necklaces. Those quippy posters we frame in our bedrooms and the motivational quotes we share on Pinterest. We still spend our cash on trophies and trinkets to declare our allegiances, after all, whether it's to the sisterhood, to politics, or to Scandinavian interior design.

We still collect stuff just for the sake of stuff, too, only now our magical corner shops are ASOS and Etsy. But really, it's online that the most devoted fan collections thrive. Gifs are our merch now. Where once we swapped photos, now it's memes and long, rambling Twitter threads, and podcasts high on their own nerdery. It's not quite the same as holding a limited edition Spice Girls Chupa Chups tin in your eager paws, but perhaps it's a natural evolution.

After all, they might be to blame for most of our historic tooth decay, but they also gave us that first taste of how nice it is to love something so unreservedly, and unironically. Without stressing over its implications for society, your purse or your personal brand. Been there, loved that, got the (unaffiliated) T-shirt.

'Listening to them now still makes me feel giddy. Like life is OK as long as I have a Chupa Chup with Emma's face on it.'

KELLY, 30

13 THINGS THAT DIDN'T LAST AS LONG AS GIRL POWER

The scar from your BCG jab

Chain letters

Every Celtic band tattoo acquired between 1996 and 2000

The Mr Frosty you got for Christmas and broke by Boxing Day

Mad cow disease

The Tamagotchi that one kid in your school managed to keep alive for three years

New Labour

Line dancing

Blue Peter bring-and-buy sales

The arms on your Stretch Armstrong

All those hexes you incurred for opening your crisp packet upside down

The Millennium bug

Peter Andre's sex appeal

'I was living in Blackburn, had just turned eight, and they were the most exciting thing I'd ever seen. Before the Spice Girls my role models were probably Disney princesses.'

SAM, 30

9

From 'Mama' to Maggie

THE SPICE GIRLS AND THE WOMEN WHO WENT BEFORE

magine this: you're the most successful female music act in the world. You've spent several months at number one, garnered thousands of fans, raked in a ton of commercial success and you've still only had three singles out. So what do you choose for your fourth? A song about the pressures of global fame, or how many yachts you're going to buy? A whispery folk ballad? A Euro-disco banger? Byron, Shelley and Keats, recited over a hip-hop beat?

Nope, you set an example for well-mannered young superstars everywhere. You thank your mum.

When you look back on it now, 'Mama' could have been so, so bad. Existing in a tiny canon of family-focused schmaltz pop along with 'There's No-one Quite Like Grandma', Clive Dunn's 'Grandad' and The Hollies' 'He Ain't Heavy, He's My Brother', it was a track with an earnest, wholesome message that seemed to go against the winking irreverence of all their other material. There was no clever wordplay or playful hidden message, it was straight-up smooshy sentiment. 'Mama, I love you. Mama, I care.' It even followed the golden rule: if you want to make people feel things, get a choir in.

But unlike St Winifred's chorus of lisping infants, 'Mama' somehow managed not to dissolve in a puddle of its own sap. It wasn't a novelty single, even if it was on a double A-side for Comic Relief. Framed as a grown-up apology for the Girls' wild adolescent years, 'Mama' was heartfelt but soulful and performed with laidback sincerity. Considering their last hit had been '2 Become 1', the whole thing smacked vaguely of phoning your mum after losing your virginity. It was sweet, but it still felt like the Spice Girls through and through.

Of the group, all but Victoria had been raised in single-parent households. And while Emma was the Spice who talked about her mum all the time in interviews (it became as much a part of her character identity as pigtails and pastels), the song was Melanie B's idea. She explains in *Real Life: Real Spice: The Official Story*, 'We wrote "Mama" when I was going through a bad phase with my mum. The sentiments are really that your mum's probably the best friend that you've got. Whether she's an over-protective mother or a bit of a landmine, she probably knows you better than yourself in some ways.'

Pop culture has always had a place for mothers, usually as the stern matriarch or the sighing family doormat. But the idea that you could be mates with your mum felt new and intriguing – especially to those of us who hadn't hit puberty yet, let alone gone through years of adolescent door-slamming. So did the idea that our mothers might actually have lived a life before we came along, rather than just popping up from flatpack in a BHS nightie and perm, ready to be handed an infant bundle. Mums, we learned from the song, might be killjoys and adversaries when it came to the fun parts of growing up, but we'd thank them in the end. Strangely, it was more convincing when the Spice Girls said it than when our mums did.

But as well as a hit, 'Mama' was also a genius PR

move. Just as the group might have been in danger of falling out of parental approval – for the skimpy outfits, the boorish behaviour and the endless parade of tabloid front pages – they went and outed themselves as a massive bunch of mother-lovers. The Spice Girls were Friends of the Mums! Parental Guidance welcomed! It hinted that under all the vamping and yelling, they might be the kind of girls who always wrote their thank-you letters on Boxing Day. How could anyone fail to be charmed?

Even my own mother, who was staunchly resistant to the idea of being her children's 'best friend' (she told me in no uncertain terms when I was about fourteen that if I ever had a hen weekend, she wouldn't come on it), found the whole thing endearing. And that's generous of her, because *circa* 1997 I was pretty much a precocious nightmare.

'I think my generation was probably finding their way a bit with parenting, because we wanted to do it very differently – particularly the mother–daughter relationship,' she said, when I phoned her to demand her take (I am still a nightmare). 'Parents in my day would see it as their right to go into your bedroom and read your diary, or make your decisions for you. I wanted to respect your boundaries.'

For those of us who needed help navigating those boundaries, 'Mama' was also the first time the Spices really tried their Big Sister role on for size. Knowing by this point what the average age of their fans was, they played to their young audience by inviting some of them along to be in the video. As well as their own mothers. Victoria wore a bikini top, which we all took as helpful evidence that bare midriffs and good daughtering weren't mutually exclusive.

In the problem page of their quarterly *SPICE* magazine, the Girls dispensed a mix of sage wisdom ('It's a very old-fashioned attitude to think it's not manly or macho to be affectionate to a girl in public,' Victoria told a fan whose boyfriend ignored her in front of his mates) and advice no licensed counsellor would ever endorse ('Personally I'd sit on his knee and grab him in front of his friends anyway!' added Mel B). They were old enough to have lived a bit, but young enough to remember how it felt. For those of us who didn't have older girls around to bridge the gap between parent and peer, the Spice Girls gamefully stepped up to the mark.

But more than just savvy marketing, this great big family love-in said something about the way the group saw themselves: as carrying a torch in a much bigger procession of women.

'Girl power's been around since the Dark Ages,' Geri once told a Finnish interviewer in 1997. 'Joan of Arc. Queen Victoria. The Suffragettes. God.'

While many of their young fans came to the idea of girl power as something irresistibly shiny and new, the Spices themselves never tried to pretend they invented it. Sure, they repackaged it, spruced it up a bit, coated it in body glitter and made it palatable to new tastes – 'feminism vamped up for the nineties', as Mel B once

What would the SPICE GIRLS do?

put it – but they knew they were part of a long, long lineage of female groundbreakers, from single mothers to cultural icons. And they were always determined to pay tribute to the women who went before.

The women who went before, however, were a little less convinced.

Vivienne Westwood laid into them on TV, which shouldn't have been so surprising – except that the Godmother of Punk's objection wasn't to their frothy bubblegum pop, it was to how they were 'corrupting the youth' with their 'disgusting behaviour'. WILL NOBODY THINK OF THE CHILDREN?

'Those Spice Girls have never had any education, they have never been brought up – they have just been allowed to grow up like animals,' she told a bemused Carol Smillie. 'Their dreadful clothes, their dreadful look and no style. They are just cultivating this attitude that you should push your way to the top – it doesn't matter if you have talent or not.'

Of course, moral outrage from the grown-ups only made the Spice Girls seem cooler. Of all people, Vivienne 'literally called my shop "SEX"' Westwood should have known that.

Elsewhere, second- and third-wave feminists struggled to know what to make of this jacuzzi of girly zeitgeist. Writer Natasha Walter confessed that she liked what the Spice Girls represented in the early days. 'It's a good sign that their generation is learning to be comfortable with their bodies and, at the same time, to speak up and be confident with their opinions and their desires,' she wrote in the *Independent*, in an article that nonetheless decided, by 2001, that their 'candy-floss version of girlpower' hadn't really achieved anything.

'I didn't realize at the time what a big impact they were having,' admits my high school French teacher, whose attempt to update her lessons with a bit of girl power failed when she accidentally called them the Spice Sisters. She recognized girl power as feminism, she says, 'but a different type to the seventies. It encouraged typically "male" bad behaviour, but not important things like equal pay and opportunities.'

'Not the important things' was a recurring theme. Through many older pairs of eyes, girl power was fun, fluffy, high-spirited hijinks – not inherently toxic, but you couldn't expect it to change anything.

Having marched and fought for all the rights we took for granted, you can see how previous generations might have despaired of us trampling all over their legacy like goats at a picnic. But there was another kind of panic too, the panic that children were growing up too fast. No sooner were we out of nappies, they feared, than we were in hot pants, going proto-Honey Boo Boo with a Geri doll in hand. The world was out to ruin the girl, and pop culture was enemy number one.

In her 1999 book *The Whole Woman*, Germaine Greer tentatively praised the Spice Girls for achieving 'an educational level not aimed at by the dead-eyed emaciated models featured in *More*', and decided that they 'did make a difference because their most passionate fans were eight-year-old girls'.

But she worried about those eight-year-olds too. 'The propaganda machine that is now aimed at our daughters is more powerful than any form of indoctrination that has ever existed before,' she warned. All those years of hard work and dogma, decrying objectification and trying to shrink the gap between the sexes, and suddenly everything was 'girls' this, 'girls' that, push-up bras, lollipops and pigtails. You can see where she might have had trouble.

But Germaine might be interested to know that on Amazon, her seminal work *The Female Eunuch* is listed under the 'Customers also bought' section for *Girl Power: The Official Book* by the Spice Girls. So perhaps they were a bigger gateway drug than she gave them credit for. And where the Spice Girls continued to stand for cheerful, broad-brush inclusivity, the same can't really be said of Greer, who in recent years has made transphobic comments and dismissed the #MeToo movement as 'whingeing'.

Thankfully, not everyone felt the Spice Girls' influence was a hollow one. The mamas, for the most part, were on board. 'My mum, a feminist writer, absolutely loved the Spice Girls and very much approved of them bringing Girl Power to the masses,' says Catriona Innes, Senior Editor at *Cosmopolitan*. 'She told me it was feminism, which I tried to tell my friends but they dismissed it and said feminism was about hairy armpits. I didn't argue.'

In that respect, the Spice Girls weren't just treading water. With their 'dreadful clothes' (honestly Vivienne, there aren't enough sideways looks to camera in the world) they were helping to unpick stereotypes that badly needed unpicking if we were going to make any more progress. The dungarees, the man-hating, the idea that liberated women couldn't enjoy a supportive underwire or a cool breeze against smoothly shaven shin, if that was their jam. The timeworn trope that said the feminine couldn't possibly be feminist, and vice versa. In the past twenty years we've chewed over the same tired 'CAN A FEMINIST HAVE A BRAZILIAN THO?' debate until it's nothing but gristle and we've still not reached a unanimous conclusion, so it's hard to get our heads round just how deeply ingrained those ideas were back in 1997.

If feminism needed new role models, the Spices were happy to take on the job. But when it came to choosing their own role models, that's where things got sticky.

You probably know this next bit. On 1 December 1996, fresh from collecting three awards at the *Smash Hits* Poll Winners Party, the Spice Girls gave an interview to Simon Sebag Montefiore for *The Spectator*. This was a weird move on all counts. *The Spectator* was (and still is) a right-wing political magazine, read mainly by ruddy-faced, red-trousered rich men. It rarely let pop stars sully its pages, unless it was to mock them or expose them saying something scandalous. If they were inviting the Spice Girls in, it could only be with one goal in mind.

Sebag Montefiore hit the back of the net. In a pre-dictably piss-takey interview headlined 'Spice Girls Back Sceptics on Europe', the Girls shared their views on the single currency, the EU, the monarchy, British constitutional reform and – you could virtually hear the *Spectator* staff rubbing their hands with glee – Margaret Thatcher. 'We Spice Girls are true Thatcherites,' declared Geri, in a quote that would soon be slapped across newspapers up and down the land, and metaphorically across her forehead for ever. 'Thatcher was the first Spice Girl, the pioneer of our ideology – Girl Power.'

Whoomp, there it is. By dropping the T-bomb, Geri had committed a sacrilege that no amount of glitter or Rimmel Hide the Blemish could conceal. As biographer David Sinclair noted, 'In the pop world there is almost no crime more heinous than being a Tory.'

The kids were largely oblivious, but suddenly the grown-ups were interested. As *The Spectator* sat back and enjoyed its biggest sales figures in 200 years, other 'serious' news outlets all raced to give the 'SPICE GIRLS ARE MASSIVE TORIES' story their own particular spin. Either way, right and left wingers alike, it mainly boiled down to gloating. See, the commentators crowed, we knew they were too sexy and popular to be empowering! It was that special brand of sexism and snobbery, the one that manages to condemn you for your opinions while somehow also deciding you're too stupid to even understand them.

Geri performed an Olympic-effort backpedal a few

months later. 'Of course, [Thatcher] destroyed a lot of things. Everyone makes mistakes and she did. She fucked up big-time loads of different things, definitely,' she told *The Face*. 'But what I give her credit for is she is the first fucking woman.'

Now, we've all said things we'd rather not have quoted back at us (I once confidently explained to a friend that 'Tory' was short for 'the Conservative Party') and mercifully, most of us only have to cope with our friends and family reminding us of our screw-ups.

But the bigger question remains: Why couldn't they admire Thatcher?

As a woman widely regarded to have smashed the glass ceiling but then pulled the ladder up after herself, Maggie was no friend to the female cause. Being a feminist and a Tory was, to many, an oxymoron. But in the simple, celebratory world of Spicedom, the logic seemed to stack up. They extolled 'girl power', she was a powerful girl. By the same merit, any woman who wore a crown or barked an order was a Spice Girl of sorts. Boudicca. Elizabeths I and II. Captain Mildred, the admiral from *Charlie Chalk*. They'd said it themselves; it was an open invite. They wanted everyone in their gang.

Whether cheering or condemning Geri's comments, the glee with which the media leapt on the Spice Girls was the same kind of glee with which outspoken women are still torn apart now. We see this ritual de-throning happen time and again with every new queen. Lena Dunham, Caitlin Moran, Amy Schumer, Caitlyn Jenner,

Taylor Swift, Erykah Badu, J. K. Rowling, Chimamanda Ngozi Adichie, Mary Berry – another day, another cancelled celebrity. The roll call grows faster than you can keep track on your Femina Non Grata spreadsheet and send back your '[INSERT BELOVED ICON] FOR QUEEN' phone case.

For as long as they're up, they're hailed as super-heroes. The future of womankind rests on their shoulders. But the first dubious comment, the first chink in the armour, any ill-formed thought or unresearched theory and instead of being calmly challenged or corrected, they're relegated to the dustbin of celebrity shame.

Which is not to say that those with a platform or privilege should never be called out on their bullshit. Of course they should. Those discussions are vital; they're how we learn, grow and push forward. But it's that feeling that the world is continually poised, with popcorn, waiting for every successful woman to slip up. It takes whole court cases to write powerful men off with the same vigour (often not even then), while a woman can be felled with a single rotten tweet.

There's a reason you rarely hear anyone described as the 'bad girl' of art/literature/music/film, the way countless men are lauded for their dodgy behaviour. Maybe, just maybe, when there are precious few female role models in the history books, the answer isn't to vilify women for looking up to the ones they have – it's to make more role models, and better role models.

Nowadays, if we want an inspiring female prime

minister, we don't need Thatcher. We can look to Jacinda Ardern of New Zealand, the world's youngest female head of government, who gave birth in June 2018 while still in office. We're slowly upgrading the early prototypes for success.

So, do the Spice Girls themselves require an upgrade, or are they firmly in the filing cabinet of time? Ginger, Baby, Scary, Sporty and Posh never started any wars or miners' strikes, unless there was a crucial issue of *Smash Hits* I missed, but somehow we're still not sure if they qualify as role models. Since I started writing this book, more than a few people in the pub have told me animatedly how much they loved the group and how inspiring they found them, before leaning in conspiratorially and saying something to the tune of 'But of course, they weren't *actually* feminists, were they?'

To them I usually say, 'You tell me!' and wiggle my eyebrows enigmatically, but to you now, I say, why must we do this? When a woman sticks her head above the parapet, why is our first instinct to catch her out and cry, 'A-HA!' as though we're discovering the giant was actually three children in a trench coat all along?

Don't get me wrong, I enjoy the hunt for Secret Feminism as much as the next modern gal with Twitter and too much time on her hands ('Is this secretly feminist?' we wonder, watching *Don't Tell the Bride*. 'Is THIS secretly feminist?' we think, paying our gas bill. 'Is THIS?!' we ask, holding up a ham sandwich and squinting), but the older I get, the more I'm inclined to think that maybe sorting things into 'feminist' and 'not feminist' isn't like sorting the recycling. There are no definitive criteria. Sometimes it feels like feminism to one person, not to the next. Sometimes you just don't know until you look back twenty years later and observe the effects.

But maybe we can agree that the Spice Girls were, at least, a starter kit. A set of training wheels, and a good strong push to get us moving. As one interviewee articulated it, better than I can, 'I guess girl power was a precursor of feminism "proper" for me. It helped instil in me the basic understanding that being a girl was a Good Thing, while becoming a feminist was realizing that not everyone thought, like me, that being a girl was a Good Thing.'

They were something else, too – a spoonful of sugar to help the doctrine go down. 'They both are and represent a voice that has too long been repressed. The voices, not really the voice, of young women and, just as important, of women not from the educated classes,' wrote Kathy Acker, one feminist foremother who really did get the point of girl power. It wasn't academic. It didn't require you to have a degree in gender studies or a house full of books to join in. It didn't tell you everything you did was wrong, or that everything you liked was toxic and needed to go on the bonfire. It was accessible, not just to kids, but to those young women that 'proper' feminism might never have reached, or scared off altogether. It went out and found them, and welcomed them in.

I think parenting expert Geethika Jayatilaka had it right in 2001, when she told an audience at the Institute of Contemporary Arts, 'Whatever you think about the Spice Girls, they showed that feminism could be repackaged and sold. Instead of looking down our noses at this phenomenon we need to think about how to harness and use it.'

Juno Dawson regards it as feminism for an age that dared not say the word. 'I know a lot of feminist academics hated the Spice Girls because they were managed by a male Svengali, they were thin and cute, but I'm not sure they were looking hard enough,' she says. 'They were young, fiercely ambitious, made a fuck-ton of money, shagged men, had babies and, vitally, made choices. It feels like they paved the way for a more modern, Caitlin Moran-esque take on feminism – girls should have all the same choices boys have. That's what the Spice Girls represented to me: they were the biggest artists in the world...and they were girls.'

If you can see it, you can be it, and for those two years in the late nineties, there was nobody more visible (or audible) than the Spice Girls. We can tie ourselves in knots over the arguments and the flawed rhetoric and the who-said-what-when until we're exhausted, but ultimately it's the women we can see that we remember. Whether she's a brilliant mum, a bad prime minister, or another guilty feminist simply having a go.

Nowadays, of course, using motherhood as a kind of golden amulet of empowerment doesn't really wash.

What about the women who can't be mothers, or don't want to be mothers? What about the girls with crap mothers, or no mothers, or two excellent dads? Every time someone starts a sentence with 'Speaking as a mother', and then goes on to say something like 'I am against murder!', it reinforces the notion that there's an extra special level of sentient womanhood we can only unlock through our wombs. Or that women were put on earth to be caretakers, mop and bucket included, while men looking after their own children is some kind of bonus extra event they can meddle in. It feels retro.

But while we're kind of done tethering our worth to our ovaries, we are in no way done giving the women who have come before us the credit they deserve for weathering everything they have. Whether that's wiping our bums, setting us boundaries or giving the glass ceiling a hearty thwack with the pointy stick of their ambition.

It doesn't mean they're always right, or that their way is the only way. But in their typically hug-it-out-ladies style, the Spice Girls made a point: that we could respect and learn from the women of previous generations, even while we kicked against their legacy. In a way, I guess, they introduced us to the notion of a 'problematic fave'. So maybe it's OK if they became one.

'I've often thought back to how lucky I was to have lived through Spicemania. To spend so much time adoring women. Women who looked relatively average, who were wild and unapologetic.'

SERENA, 30

15 CANDIDATES FOR THE SIXTH SPICE GIRL

Mrs Merton

Katie Hill

Konnie Huq

Romana, the other *Blue Peter* presenter nobody remembers

The Vicar of Dibley

The real-life vicar the Vicar of Dibley was based on

Morag, the cow from *Fully Booked*

Lily Savage

Mulan

That one cool, young teacher who used to just let you watch a video in Geography

Mel C's gold tooth

The talking head from *Art Attack*

Mrs Doubtfire

Dolly the sheep

You

'I am having a baby girl this year, and am sad that she won't grow up with the Spice Girls' influence instead of what's on offer today.'

AMY, 32

10

Chicas to the front

THE SPICE GIRLS AND THE WOMEN WHO COME NEXT

'It's not a coincidence, you know.'

That's what I've been told again and again, when asking women my age about the Spice Girls. With even more regularity than anecdotes about hair mascara (it turns out hair mascara really left its mark on us, both physically and metaphorically), they've wanted to tell me it wasn't a coincidence that the generation who grew up with girl power is the generation who ushered in the fourth wave of feminism. It wasn't just a bit of girlish fun, although it *was* so much fun; it was also a catalyst for something bigger. If what the Spice Girls gave us was a feminist starter kit, then plenty of us later went out and bought the whole damn lifestyle.

'It's quite nice that now, as an adult, for the most part I'm not looking back and thinking, "Oh my God, it's so embarrassing, the scales have fallen from my eyes…"' said Otegha Uwagba with palpable relief, because there aren't many cultural relics from a nineties childhood that we can revisit without wincing at the sheer wokeless-ness of it all. 'Actually, they were ahead of their time in many ways and doing things that a lot of people since haven't managed to do.'

There are plenty of things we *have* managed to do, though. The girl power generation is slogging away – challenging norms, changing laws, hollering back. A 2018 report concluded that young women today are more politically and socially engaged than young men, more likely to participate in activism, and twice as likely to see LGBTQ+ rights and gender equality as critical issues (though that last one is hardly a shock).

But is it just wishful thinking to imagine the Spice Girls had any part in galvanizing us? Is it like at school, when you demanded to know if Shakespeare *really* meant all this symbolism when he wrote it, or did he just think the words sounded good?

Truth is, I don't know. Correlation doesn't prove causation, I know that much. That's one thing I did learn in school. Sometimes everyone just gets the same idea at the same time – like the year of the side fringe, or when everybody started using 'immense' as a catch-all descriptor.

But even if we're never going to be able to draw a felt-tip line directly from 'Wannabe' to the #MeToo movement and confidently say 'ta-da', all that high-kicking, outspoken attitude had to go somewhere. We certainly didn't use it all up on nu rave. And while the Spice Girls may have been part of a movement much bigger than themselves, young girls would find it hard to remember anything that had a stronger influence or a wider reach during those formative years than the Girls did.

'I think culturally the Spice Girls were a key part of a journey for many women who are now in their late twenties or early thirties,' says Ashley Fryer, who did her own bit for rallying the troops when she founded the Awesome Women of Twitter. 'We're in the midst of changes in the way the world sees and treats women, and I think the early influences on our generation can't be ignored. It's very possible that girl power played a part in that shift for many of us.'

Natasha Walter once wrote that the Spice Girls' iteration of girl power was a positive thing, 'so long as you took it for what it was and didn't expect a Mars Bar to be a full meal'. It's a handy analogy, because while a Mars Bar isn't nutritionally complete, what it will give you is an energy boost. A Mars Bar is also more delicious than, say, a kale salad – and perhaps the reason girl power elicits such fond memories for us today is because it felt like a treat, not a chore.

Kathy Acker had it right when she ended her 1997 *Guardian* profile of the group by announcing it was up to feminism to take on board the Spice Girls' contribution and 'keep on transforming society as society is best transformed, with lightness and in joy'.

The transformation is far from complete, the joy we're still working on, but the lightness we're managing nicely. 'High' and 'low' culture are more interwoven than ever. We punctuate our political rants with quotes from *Love Actually,* then tear *Love Actually* apart for its politics. There has been a slew of sassy, progressive sitcoms, your *Crazy Ex-Girlfriend*s and *Brooklyn Nine-Nine*s and *The Good Place*s, and we're bingeing on them freely and debating them like books afterwards. *RuPaul's Drag Race* and *Queer Eye* are both challenging gender convention and helping to push LGBTQ+ culture to a place of mainstream adoration.

This year, *Love Island* has sparked important national conversations around consent, slut-shaming and emotional abuse. Beyoncé and Jay-Z filled the Louvre with fresh meaning, and in turn their 'Apeshit' video was appraised like high art. *Oceans 8* has proved that a female-fronted heist movie can fill cinemas, and it doesn't even have to be that good. An actress has come to save the royal family from irrelevance. I don't know what any of this means, exactly, except, don't underestimate pop culture. Don't underestimate the things girls like.

And while we're at it, don't underestimate girls.

Let's think more about the 'girls' thing, shall we? Every time I've written 'the Girls' in this book, I've felt a funny, subversive little jolt. Being called a 'girl' when you're a fully grown woman is sometimes benign, sweet even, but sometimes it stings like a slap.

After all, you've earned that adulthood. You've learned so much and worked so hard, just existing in this world, that to have it all stripped away with one syllable feels like being cruelly short-changed. In my last office job, I was routinely referred to as a 'girl' by a boss four years younger than me, and it never stopped making me want to staple him to the desk by his balls. (Conversely, I don't know at what age it stops feeling bizarre to be referred to as a 'lady' by a parent to their child – 'Move out of the lady's way!' – but my best guess is forty-five.)

At its worst, calling grown women 'girls' belongs to the same camp as school-uniform discos: creepy, infantilizing, a way for society to belittle us and take away our power. Or else it turns women into a faceless, squealing gaggle – brunch with the girls! Girls' night out! 'Here Come The Girls!' Either way, feminist convention decrees we reject it.

Sonic Youth's Kim Gordon called the Spice Girls 'something out of Disneyland' in a 1997 interview with *Rolling Stone*. 'No one talks about woman power,' she said. 'They're masquerading as little girls. It's repulsive.' But as we know, feminist convention had little truck with the Spice Girls. They could call themselves girls and it was fine, because their vision of womanhood *was* young, it *was* loud, it was a vehicle for fun and glitter and an unashamed playground pack mentality. And while they were adult women (just – Emma celebrated her twenty-first birthday at the height of Spicemania with a huge glitzy party at London's Atlantic Bar; years later I celebrated mine by waking up on the landing of my student house-share with my false eyelashes stuck to the wall), they were always ringleaders for the next generation. 'Next phase, next stage, next craze, next wave.'

'We are really proud to have an audience of younger children, because they're not corrupted by anything,' Emma once said. 'They don't think, "Oh, hip hop's cool, or soul, so therefore I'm going to like it." They just hear something and they like it and that's that.' Children make the most discerning critics, they say – and when you consider that the adult audiences of 1996 sent Celine Dion to number one four times in a year, it's hard to argue – but what they also are is loyal and uncynical. Ready to be entirely consumed by devotion. And that hasn't changed, though plenty else has.

You've got to wonder how the Spice Girls fandom might have looked in the same frenzied, digital era as

One Direction. Would we have been shipping Posh and Scary as a clandestine couple? Tweeting Geri about our dead cat? Trying to prove that Baby was really a doll all along? It'd be *wild*. But while nineties pop culture was steeped in plenty of its own conspiracy theories (Britney Spears was under the control of the Bush administration! Everyone was under control of the Illuminati! Kel from *Kenan and Kel* was dead, again!), it was hard to speculate too much about the Spice Girls – at least in the pre-Gexit years. They were just so damned honest, all of the time. The original definition of no-filter, we felt we knew everything about them.

Twenty years later, we're supposed to know everything about everyone. Social media has given today's kids more access to their celebrity heroes than ever, but in return they're living their lives on show too. Humdrum honesty isn't *de rigueur* any more. You either have to be flawless, glossy, living your best #blessed life in a rose-pink, peony-strewn, neon-lit dreamscape – or else you have to be raw, hyperreal, perpetually wrecked with anxiety and hammering out a brave confessional through your tears. The really successful Instagram accounts do both. Perfection with a side of impossible pressure. Plus brunch!

I wouldn't want to be a girl today. That's the kind of thing we say, isn't it, sitting round with our tumblers of wine in our millennial mid-price pizza joints. Not that it was easy in our day, mind (I am thirty now and so I say things like 'in my day', and 'mind'), and especially not for anyone who didn't fit into the neat, white, straight, cis, able-bodied, healthy-brained, slim, clear-skinned top strata of privilege. But, wow. Doesn't modern girlhood look difficult?

This is something of a departure from previous generations, who tended to think each subsequent batch of women had a cushy sitch compared to their own. Our mums had perms and power suits, and bosses slapping them on the arse as they made the coffee. Their mums had a war. But when my generation look at the girls growing up after us, in some ways it feels like we never had it so good. Modern girlhood looks like a constant challenge.

Young girls today have to deal with so much, not least being told how much they're dealing with all the time. Research paints a picture of a generation bombarded with both obstacles and expectations. Sixty-four per cent of girls aged thirteen to twenty-one have experienced sexual harassment at school in the past year – a figure that's increased 5 per cent since 2014. Fifty-four per cent have seen graphic images online that upset them, two-thirds feel pressured to send nude photos. One-third of girls aged seven to ten think their appearance is the most important thing about them. A quarter of the same age group feel they need to be perfect. The stats come thick and fast, and with it the worry.

Yet while the millennials still feel like teenagers, wondering how to jump-start our own 'suspended adulthood', girlhood seems to be under reconstruction.

It's impossible to go back to a time of petticoated innocence – but instead, girls are beginning to learn they can order off-menu and choose something different from what they've been offered.

In many places and for millions of girls, this is as basic and as brutal as asking for the education and autonomy denied them. It's runaway child brides and FGM protestors, braver and more resilient than most of us can even comprehend. It's Malala Yousafzai, standing up to be shot in the head for her right to go to school.

But it's also the smaller, everyday things. It's the shifting focus from all the things little girls can't and shouldn't do, to all the things they can and could.

In the Western world, advertisers have picked up on this wind change, and discovered it isn't only sex that sells – female empowerment does too! Though anyone who spent their pocket money on Spice Girls crisps could have told you that. Always' 2014 viral 'Like A Girl' ad campaign was a shrewd piece of marketing, but it was welcomed with open arms because it amplified an important message. More ads followed, and more articles, and more conversations, and gradually we've started putting girls front and centre more often – or at least stopped relegating them to the subs bench.

There's still a way to go, of course. On the car journey to true equality, we have barely reached the first service station loo stop. We're still having to explain that while feminism doesn't have to be a serious, scary, intellectual business, it does have to be a little bit more than just

'Wooo, LADIES!' followed by a party-blower toot noise. There's more to it than just saying, 'I love women! Look at all these women I know!' no matter how many male Hollywood stars remain convinced that all it takes to be a feminist ally is to have a) a mother, b) a daughter, c) a wife they haven't divorced yet, or d) a conversation with Meryl Streep one time at Nobu.

Society is making decent progress on the idea of women and girls being able to do 'boyish' things well – throwing, kicking, running companies and countries – and yet we still dismiss the traditionally girlish things as stupid and trivial. It's the reason we talk about 'fangirls', not just fans. Appreciating something makes you a fan, but breathless devotion makes you a fan*girl*. A hysterical mutation. It's also the reason I mute the theme music when I watch *Sex and the City* with the windows open, so my downstairs neighbours don't judge me.

And while I suppose it's nice that society is crushing on 'strong' women (it's an improvement on the days we couldn't be trusted to ride a bike without our wombs falling out), the trouble is that when people say 'strong', often what they really mean is 'showing no visible emotion'. They mean women who swallow their feelings and grit their teeth, i.e. the way men are conditioned to. If we want to be taken seriously, we're still meant to mimic the boys – which makes no sense, because, with increasingly bleak statistics emerging about the mental health of young men (suicide is the biggest single killer of men under forty-five in the UK, and around 75 per cent of all suicides are male) we know the boys aren't doing too well out of it.

'We believe that there is a cultural barrier preventing men from seeking help as they are expected to be in control at all times, and failure to be seen as such equates to weakness and a loss of masculinity,' says male suicide prevention charity CALM, the Campaign Against Living Miserably. So if we know masculine 'strength' is a shonky mould, then why do we keep on using it? Celebrating strong, smart, sassy women is wonderful, but what about the weak ones? The shy ones? The moody ones? The dumb ones who speak their mind anyway? The women who can't do a backflip, no matter how many times they hurl themselves into a sea of sofa cushions? Don't we all deserve a seat at the table, and a piece of the pie? The Spice Girls said we did, and we grew up believing them.

Liberation is still as laden with paradox as it was in the nineties.

Take periods. On the one hand, we're arguing for them not to hold us back. They're natural, not shameful. They're not a horror movie situation and they're certainly no reason to discriminate against people who have them. Anything you can do, we can do bleeding! But on the other hand … we can't, not always. Not everyone. When you're blighted by cramps for several days a month, or crippled by a condition such as endometriosis, or if the hyena pack of hormones stampeding round your body is making you anxious and teary and exhausted, and slumping over a four-pack of soft cookies is still more of a challenge than you're up to, we need that experience recognized and respected. We need medical research and sick leave and, above all, access to sanitary supplies, because we never asked for our bodies to be a battleground. Periods are no big deal, except when they are. Women are as hard as nails, but we shouldn't always have to be.

Likewise we have to be ruthless, but also compassionate. Sexy but not slutty. Sex-positive, but not objectified. We have to remind the world that although 'women helping women' is a lovely mantra, it doesn't mean men are off the hook. Although we want to project-manage our own liberation, it shouldn't always be down to us to make change happen. It's bloody exhausting. Ginger Rogers once famously asserted that everything Fred Astaire did she had done 'backwards, in heels'. Twenty-first-century girlhood often feels like dancing backwards in heels while also selling the programmes and running the snack kiosk.

But while we worry about them, the girls themselves are rolling up their sleeves and getting on with the job. They're fixing things. Cheerfully, energetically, angrily, impatiently, brilliantly. They're multitasking like demons, even though they shouldn't have to. The annual Girls' Attitudes Survey by Girlguiding tells us that 95 per cent of girls between the ages of eleven and twenty-one want more positive, diverse representations of girls and women in advertising. Two-thirds feel confident confronting sexual harassers at school. Fifty-eight per cent think the voting age should be lowered to sixteen. And even before they have democratic power in their hands, they're agitating for change.

Whenever I need to be reassured that the world isn't going to hell in a Handmaid's basket bag, I think about girls like Amika George. In April 2017, aged seventeen, she founded the #FreePeriods campaign, after reading that there were girls in Leeds missing school every month because they couldn't afford pads and tampons. A child of the internet, she did what came naturally: she started a hashtag, an online petition and an IRL revolt.

By December the same year, together with The Pink Protest, a collective of thoroughly modern young activists founded by Scarlett Curtis, Grace Campbell and Alice Skinner (slogan: 'The revolution will be pink and posted on Instagram'), George had organized a 2,000-strong protest at Downing Street and secured £1.5 million from the government to address UK period poverty. In eight months, girls had done what the adults had been meaning to get round to for years. And they'd shown that while social media might cause problems for today's teens, it also offers solutions on a bigger scale than ever before.

'I am lobbying the government, and they need to listen because the shouts are getting louder and louder for change,' Amika tells me, the day after finishing her A-Levels. 'My ultimate goal is for every child to be able to access menstrual products when they need them. Things are changing, slowly, and I'm really confident that we will make real inroads into debunking period taboos in a determined and fearless way.'

Fearless is the word that comes up again and again with today's girls. It's even been immortalized, in Kristen Visbal's bronze statue of the *Fearless Girl*, hands on hips, defiant, which stared down the *Charging Bull* of Wall Street in New York's financial district for a year (although, funded by a corporate investment firm, she stared down plenty of critics too). And while, like the anxious millennials, Gen Z is far from peachy on an individual level, they're finding that fearlessness in numbers. As the critics drone louder about the narcissism of youth than they did in the nineties, the girl gangs are back again to prove them wrong.

Body positivity is another long overdue uprising, and one we definitely can't pretend the Spice Girls started – although knowing now that several of the group were suffering with eating disorders during the height of their fame, they might have been glad of it too. As one grown-up Sporty fan lamented, 'To think that I was judging myself next to a woman who was barely eating makes me so sad.'

Today's #BoPo movement isn't perfect yet (rather than flaunting our 'flaws', people are beginning to ask, wouldn't it be a bigger relief to just stop talking about our bodies altogether?), but still, how I wish with every fibre of my being that it had come along sooner. How different might my teenage years have been if I'd been able to scroll through soft bellies in bikinis, thighs dappled with cellulite and unfiltered, acne-scarred skin? How many fewer hours would I have wasted crying into my SlimFast because I was fat and *ipso facto* unfanciable?

When I was growing up we never really had famous girls our age to look up to, outside of Charlotte Church and the Olsen twins – it's partly why honorary girls like the Spice Girls had such an impact. But now, thanks to the internet, the fearless girls just keep on coming. Girls such as Emma González, the gun control activist who rallied one of the largest student protests in history after her classmates were massacred in the 2018 Parkland school shooting. Yara Shahidi, founder of Eighteen x '18, a creative platform designed to encourage more young people to vote. Jazz Jennings, the seventeen-year-old transgender activist with a 500k-strong YouTube following, or Teddy Quinlivan, the model who is refusing to work with photographers accused of sexual assault. Millie Bobby Brown, Amandla Stenberg, SZA, every teen starlet using the red carpet to talk about their views, not their shoes. Like the girls incorporating protest messages into their nail art, or the young women in China who are using emojis to sidestep state censorship and share their #MeToo stories (they use a bowl of rice and a bunny, because the characters for 'rice bunny' are pronounced 'mi tu').

That scrappy DIY resourcefulness has been part of girl culture for years. Necessity is the mother of invention, and maybe the daughter too.

Online, girls' genius and creativity also gets the audience it's always deserved. And oh, I love them all. I love the teens responding to requests for naked photos with shower selfies in goofy umbrella hats, or by unveiling a series of never-ending towels. I love the Tweeter currently reminding everyone on my feed about Donald Trump's immigration policy, that 'the world is literally a planet NO ONE owns'. I love the fact that no matter how bleak things get, no matter how arid and apocalyptic the landscape of female experience seems to look, that gleeful, sparky silliness never dies. Girls will wave a fist with one hand and craft a perfect meme with the other.

And now, when I call my adult friends 'girls' (or 'gals', 'gurls', 'gewls', not sorry), that's the thrill it gives me. It makes me feel like I'm part of a force so much bigger than myself, and one that stretches far, far into the future.

I asked Amika George what her generation needs to keep its momentum going, and the answer was a familiar one. 'We need to have more self-belief. We need to be less cautious, more feisty, less afraid of being judged. We really need to understand that age should never stop us from achieving what we want, and that when we come together as a group and really support each other, we make amazing things happen.'

Less cautious, more feisty, more confident, less afraid, finding power in a group...Remind you of anything?

There's a popular theory which says it takes roughly twenty years for a particular fashion trend to start looking cool again. Chewing gum takes seven years to leave your system; cowboy boots, pedal pushers and hanky-hemmed paisley skirts take twenty. It's science. And

What would the SPICE GIRLS do?

it makes sense that the same is probably true of pop icons. It's the reason everyone got very into ABBA just before the millennium.

Do you remember that? For a few years in the nineties, ABBA were everything. Listen to Steps' back catalogue now and it sounds like Sweden's Eurovision reject pile being sung by a sat-nav. In fact, back then, ABBA's *Gold* was the only album I caned nearly as much as *Spiceworld*. My parents, who had raised us on a careful diet of Van Morrison, Paul Simon and Carole King, were baffled. But twenty years had lapsed and them's the rules.

All of which must mean that the time is ripe for a full-blown Spice Girls revival. Now that they've served their two decades in the musical wilderness, it's time for a new generation to fall in love with Scary, Baby, Sporty, Ginger and Posh the way we did.

But does it still *need* them the way we did?

It's so tempting to say yes, of course. To say that with a proper intersectional update, more diversity and more savvy media training, the Spice Girls' vision of girl power could be better than ever. Such a pithy note to end a book on, don't you think?

But I'm not going to, because the truth is, tomorrow's kids don't need our hand-me-down revolutions. They'll keep on the way we did, picking and choosing, finding their own heroes, re-evaluating the world around them and reinventing their feminism to fit it.

And I am so excited to watch that happen. I am

excited to be the old lady with her ginger wig on backwards, smelling of vanilla and tangerine and sour cream and chive, who pinches their cheeks at the bus stop and tells them they remind her of herself at their age. Back when all she wanted was to start a brilliant gang, do a killer dance routine, laugh, shout, run about, goad a Gallagher brother, wear the stupidest shoes she could find and give the patriarchy a good kicking.

The kids will look unimpressed and fly off in their hovering space pods, because that's kids for you. But I won't mind.

And as for us, my millennial women, the girl power generation? We'll probably love them for ever. Deeply, passionately, problematically, whatever. You might not see many of us in a Union Jack dress again any time soon (curses, Brexit), but all it takes is 2.29 seconds for the most recognizable cackle in pop music to rouse us, like a siren, and remind us of everything girl power made us feel and everything we wanted to achieve with it. It was a rallying cry back then, and it still echoes just as loud within us today. People can say it was all nonsense if they like, but we know differently. We know it meant something.

Apart from 'zig-a-zig-ah'. In hindsight, that might have been bollocks.

Spice up your reading!
A BIBLIOGRAPHY

BOOKS
Dawson, Juno, *The Gender Games: The Problem with Men and Women, from Someone Who Has Been Both* (Two Roads, 2018)
Fielding, Helen, *Bridget Jones's Diary* (Picador, 1996)
Hibberd, Jessamy and Usmar, Jo, *This Book Will Make You Confident* (Quercus, 2014)
Hopkins, Susan, *Girl Heroes: The New Force in Popular Culture* (Pluto Press, 2002)
Orenstein, Peggy, *Girls & Sex: Navigating the Complicated New Landscape* (Oneworld, 2016)
Roupenian, Kristen, *Cat Person* (Jonathan Cape, 2018)
Sinclair, David, *Wannabe: How the Spice Girls Reinvented Pop Fame* (Omnibus Press, 2004)
Spice Girls, *Real Life: Real Spice: The Official Story* (Zone/Chameleon, 1997)
Uwagba, Otegha, *Little Black Book: A Toolkit for Working Women* (Fourth Estate, 2017)

PRINT MEDIA
Acker, Kathy, 'All Girls Together', *Guardian*, May 1997
Bikini Kill, *Girl Power*, 1991
Hattenstone, Simon, 'Bye-bye Baby', *Guardian*, 18 November 2006
Heath, Chris, 'Spice: Above and Beyond', *The Face*, March 1997

Heath, Chris, 'Spice Girls: Too Hot to Handle', *Rolling Stone*,
    July 1997
Sebag Montefiore, Simon, 'Spice Girls Back Sceptics on Europe',
    The Spectator, 14 December 1996
SPICE, Issue 4 (John Brown Content Publishing, 1997)

ONLINE MEDIA
Lodge, Alex, *Spice Girls: 20 Years of Spice*, 2016, YouTube
www.gal-dem.com

TV
Davis, Neil, *Raw Spice*, 2001, Zig Zag Productions

PODCASTS
Unpopped: The Spice Girls and Kathy Acker, BBC Podcasts,
    26 February 2018
RuPaul: What's the Tee? with Michelle Visage, episode 140 – Emma
    Bunton, The Paragon Collective LLC, 28 February 2018

Songs referenced in the book

'Spice Up Your Life', Spice Girls (Spice Girls, Rowe, Matt and
    Stannard, Richard). *Spiceworld*, Virgin, 1997.
'Too Much', Spice Girls (Spice Girls, Watkins, Andy and Wilson, Paul).
    Spiceworld, Virgin, 1997.
'The Lady Is a Vamp', Spice Girls (Spice Girls, Watkins, Andy and
    Wilson, Paul). *Spiceworld*, Virgin, 1997.
'Wannabe', Spice Girls (Spice Girls, Rowe, Matt and Stannard,
    Richard). *Spice*, Virgin, 1996.
'Who Do You Think You Are', Spice Girls (Spice Girls, Watkins, Andy
    and Wilson, Paul). *Spice*, Virgin, 1996.
'2 Become 1', Spice Girls (Spice Girls, Rowe, Matt and Stannard,
    Richard). *Spice*, Virgin, 1996.
'Girl Power', Shampoo (Askew, Caroline, Fitzpatrick, Conall and Blake,
    Jacqui). *Girl Power*, Food, 1995.
'Love Thing', Spice Girls (Spice Girls, Kennedy, Eliot, Bayliss, Cary).
    Spice, Virgin, 1996.
'Do It', Spice Girls (Spice Girls, Watkins, Andy and Wilson, Paul).
    Spiceworld, Virgin, 1997.

'Last Time Lover', Spice Girls (Spice Girls, Watkins, Andy and Wilson, Paul). *Spice*, Virgin, 1996.

'Something Kinda Funny', Spice Girls (Spice Girls, Watkins, Andy and Wilson, Paul). *Spice*, Virgin, 1996.

'Naked', Spice Girls (Spice Girls, Watkins, Andy and Wilson, Paul). *Spice*, Virgin, 1996.

'If U Can't Dance', Spice Girls (Spice Girls, Rowe, Matt and Stannard, Richard). *Spice*, Virgin, 1996.

'Stop', Spice Girls (Spice Girls, Watkins, Andy and Wilson, Paul). *Spiceworld*, Virgin, 1997.

'Whole Again', Atomic Kitten (Kershaw, Stuart, McCluskey, Andy, Padley, Bill and Godfrey, Jem). *Right Now*, Virgin, 2001.

'Born to Make You Happy', Britney Spears (Lundin, Kristian and Carlsson, Andreas). *...Baby One More Time*, Jive, 1999.

'What Can I Do', The Corrs (Corr, Andrea, Corr, Caroline, Corr, Jim, Corr, Sharon). *Talk On Corners*, Atlantic, Lava, 143 Records, 1997.

'How Do I Live', LeAnn Rimes (Warren, Diane). *You Light Up My Life: Inspirational Songs*, Curb, 1997.

'Love Fool', The Cardigans (Persson, Nina, Svensson, Peter). *First Band on the Moon*, Stockholm/Mercury, 1996.

'Torn', Natalie Imbruglia (Cutler, Scott, Preven, Anne, Thornalley, Phil). *Left of the Middle*, RCA, 1997.

'Doing Me', Ray BLK (Kushka, Gina and Ekwere, Rita Ifiok Abasi). Island, 2017.

'Supercalifragilisticexpialidocious', Julie Andrews and Dick Van Dyke (Sherman, Robert B. and Sherman, Richard M). *Mary Poppins*, Disney, 1964.

'Parklife', Blur (Albarn, Damon, Coxon, Graham, James, Alex and Rowntree, Dave). *Parklife*, Food, 1994.

'Sound Off', Spice Girls. As featured in *Spice World*, 1997.

'Goodbye', Spice Girls (Spice Girls, Rowe, Matt and Stannard, Richard). *Forever*, Virgin, 1998.

'Never Ever', All Saints (Lewis, Shaznay, Jazayeri, Robert and Mather, Sean). *All Saints*, London Records, 1997.

'Viva Forever', Spice Girls (Spice Girls, Rowe, Matt and Stannard, Richard). *Spiceworld*, Virgin, 1997.

'These Words', Natasha Bedingfield (Bedingfield, Natasha, Kipner, Steve, Frampton, Andrew and Wilkins, Wayne). *Unwritten*, Phonogenic, 2004.

'Mama', Spice Girls (Spice Girls, Rowe, Matt and Stannard, Richard). *Spice*, Virgin, 1996.

'Move Over', Spice Girls (Spice Girls, Lane, Clifford and Wood, Mary). *Spiceworld*, Virgin, 1997.

Thank you very much

I knew that it wouldn't be enough to base this book on my own memories, thoughts and opinions (who do I think I am?), so I'm incredibly grateful to the many, many grown-up fans who took the time to share theirs with me. Thank you. I wish I had space to include every single story. The nineties were *wild*.

Thanks especially to Juno Dawson, Otegha Uwagba, Joe Stone, Alice Vincent, Nick Levine, Amika George, Dr Jessamy Hibberd, James Freedman and Alan Smith-Allison for giving me your expert insights. I really hope I did them justice. And thank you to David Sinclair, for writing the definitive Spice Girls biography and making this whole process a million times easier.

Huge thanks to my brilliant editor, Darcy Nicholson, for handing me this whole idea, letting me run amok with it, and then patiently, cleverly, helping me turn it into something readable. Every little thing you said and did was right for me. Thanks to Rebecca Wright for leaving my maddest jokes in, and taking all the clanging errors out. Thank you too to Beci Kelly for the cover of my dreams, Hannah Bright and Sophie Bruce for being better marketeers than Simon Fuller, and everyone at Transworld for treating a little book about the Spice Girls with all the passion and enthusiasm of a thousand-page literary epic.

Speaking of passion and enthusiasm, I'm so grateful to have Jemima Forrester as an agent, not to mention occasional life coach. Thank you for working so hard on my behalf, for always wanting to share the small plates and for believing I could be more than just a wannabe author.

I'm bloody lucky to have so many excellent women around me. It's *almost* like girl power wasn't just a marketing ploy.

To Daisy Buchanan, my *Schmancy* sister, thank you for being both my favourite writer and most tireless cheerleader. Without your wisdom, wit and identical reserve of niche pop cultural reference points, I'd have sacked off all this years ago. To Amy Jones and Ashley Fryer, you noble land mermaids, thank you for being a constant source of encouragement in my pocket. Thanks to Becca Caddy, Angela Clarke, Caroline Jones, Helena Hamilton, Lily Peschardt, Siam Goorwich, Sarah Raphael, Catriona Innes, Sam Baker, and plenty more writers, editors, followers and friends, for your advice and support – and for saying, 'Yeah, can't wait to read that!' whether you meant it or not.

Thank you to my Ace Gang, for eighteen solid years of love and delight. If this book sells a million copies I'll build us the snail house.

Thanks to everybody at Velasquez and Van Wezel in Crouch End, for being the greatest 'coffice' in London and never minding when I sat there for four hours, drinking one long black.

Sincere apologies to the legendary actress Celia Imrie, whom I accidentally tripped with my laptop cable while writing this book in a theatre bar. Thank you for not breaking a hip and suing me.

To my wonderful parents, thank you for letting me be a gobby little upstart in unsuitable shoes, and for making me feel like there was nothing in the world I couldn't do. Thanks to my lovely brothers, for joining in the dance routines and having far better taste in everything than me, still. Thanks to my grandmothers, past and present, for teaching me that when it comes to sartorial flamboyance, there is simply no such thing as 'too much'.

To Matt, whom I would call my Spice Boy if that didn't mean something entirely different, thank you for saying you'll be there and always, always meaning it. You're the best.

Thank you to all the activists out there fighting for gender equality, and every other kind of equality, every single day. There is still so much work to be done, but I'm filled with hope by those powering through it around the world. Support your local girl gang. Or start one.

And finally, the biggest, bounciest thank you to Geri, Emma, Mel B, Mel C and Victoria, for everything. It was a blast.

What would the SPICE GIRLS do?